LIQUIDATING AN ESTATE

How to Sell a Lifetime of Stuff, Make Some Cash, and Live to Tell About It

Martin Codina

Published by

Krause Publications, a division of F+W Media, Inc.
700 East State Street • Iola, WI 54990-0001
715-445-2214 • 888-457-2873
www.krausebooks.com

To order books or other products call toll-free 1-800-258-0929
or visit us online at www.krausebooks.com

Shutterstock photos are copyright of the following: P. 109, viviamo;
P. 203, Ralf Broskvar; P. 259, Gunnar Pippel.

ISBN-13: 978-1-4402-3665-5
ISBN-10: 1-4402-3665-8

Design by Sharon Bartsch
Edited by Kristine Manty

Printed in China

I dedicate this book to Valetta Ciarla-Codina, my wife and business partner, by whose graceful, wise and steady efforts, my little corner of the Estate Sales World became so much brighter.

Acknowledgments

Karen Lundberg Moore: My aunt, the bright funny and engaging angel of my youth, for without her caring guidance, I may well have been lost.

Don Pinard, who helped me open my first thrift shop, which was called Martin's Drifty Thrift Shop, in the mid-1970s.

Rodney Beecher Roberts, one of my first antiques consultants, always was so modest, but his brilliance showed through like the ever present twinkle in his eye.

Patricia Saultman was the best sort of appraiser an aspiring estate liquidator might ever have found, one who was so very intelligent, as well as charming.

Susan Hall, my first client; little did either of us know the career that would start, flower and flourish by her acceptance of my humble proposal.

Katherine Codina, my incredible daughter who has been working in the business with me since she was 14. The stories she could tell of treasures found would fill her own book.

Christopher Albanese, the first true blue high-end dealer I ever met. Did he drive me crazy with his dazzling depth of knowledge? Yes, as a fact he did. And I sincerely thank him for it.

My family, each of them, through their many sincere efforts, showed just how much they believed in me. Thank you Dad, Mom, Carlos, Mary, George, Lenny and Gloria for being there.

My staff: Lesley Paploa, who is a true and wonderful force of nature; Heiko Adler, who is a wealth of knowledge, as well as an overall good guy; and Andy and Vina Smith, who have always approached all of their efforts on behalf of our company as if they were dedicated owners...

Other estate liquidators: Cari Cucksey for taking the time out of her amazingly busy schedule to write the foreword to this book; Elena Symonds, and her son Guy Thomas, the owners of Quality First Estate Sales for their encouragement; Jordan Goodman of Sweet Home Estate Liquidation for his sense of humor; Rachel Fitch of Fitch Estate Sales in Austin, Texas, for her candor and sharing of knowledge; Todd Hughes of Hughes Estate Sales in Pasadena for his modeling of a high-end estate sales company, and to the many other estate liquidators who have reached out to me and given me so much.

Contents

Foreword

by Cari Cucksey

MARTIN IS A KINDRED ESTATE SALE SPIRIT. Like me, he lives, eats and breathes estate sales. While his business is located on the West Coast and mine is in the Midwest, our clients' needs are the same. No matter where the clients live, they all ask the same question … "What do we do with all this stuff?!"

Cari Cucksey

Not a day goes by that I don't receive a phone call or email from someone looking for assistance with liquidating possessions, whether their own or those belonging to parents or loved ones. With the large numbers of baby boomers and their aging parents, the need for estate sales is steadily on the rise. Each year, more and more folks need help and direction with the overwhelming task of liquidating possessions.

Based on nearly two decades of first-hand experience and expertise, Martin shares the dos and don'ts, hows and whys, ups and downs and ins and outs of the estate sale process and the growing business of estate sales.

He gets to the nitty-gritty of estate sales from start to finish. Oh, how I wish I had this book when I started my business! Stashed in the pages you will find everything from dealing with emotional stuff attachment, to determining junk vs. treasure, to knowing the difference between hoarding and collecting.

Whether you are looking for an estate sale professional or wanting to learn more about the estate sale business, this book will provide new insights into the booming world of estate sales. After reading this book, I guarantee estate sale signs will take on a whole new meaning. Watch out! You may be inspired to stop and shop and be on your way to becoming a "RePurposer'" just like me! I hope you do.

Cari Cucksey is the host of the network television hit show, "Cash & Cari," which airs on HGTV, the W Network, Choice TV and the History Channel in countries around the world. She is also an antiques matchmaker who runs RePurpose Estate Services and the RePurpose Shop in Michigan, www.repurposeshop.com.

Introduction

Whether it's due to the loss of a loved one, divorce, downsizing, or moving, an increasing number of people are having to deal with all of the stuff that's left behind.

ESTATE ❧ SA

FINE ESTATE LIQUIDATION, INC
415-235-7238   WWW.FINESF.COM

WHY A BOOK ABOUT the estate sales and estate liquidation business?

Even though this business is massively large—a complex and multifaceted industry employing thousands of people—there are still millions of people out there who have no idea what an estate sale is. Whoa, hold the press. How is that even possible? After all, what I am writing about here and what you will be learning about within the pages of this book is a multi-billion-dollar business dedicated to respectfully selling the countless objects to be found in the homes of the recently deceased or the personal property left behind after a divorce or relocation.

There are countless reasons for this, but the two that come to mind for this sad state of affairs is that most estate liquidators are time constrained; they're just too busy to get the word out and many of them don't even have websites. It's hard work to organize and sell a lifetime of accumulations on behalf of someone else. Staging and conducting an estate sale is like having to invent and then solve a different Rubik's Cube every day. It's not uncommon for an estate liquidator to work 12 hours a day seven days a week.

The second major reason for this industry to fly so low under the radar is that estate liquidators are so competitive with each other that they have never gathered together long enough in one place to share with each other what is so vital and/or successful about their estate sales methods. Estate liquidators keep to themselves because they think that to share their tactics or strategies with their competitors would mean they could lose their competitive edge.

So their collective intelligence or the vital might and muscle of their vast storehouse of experience has to date never been formed into a trade group or association. The net effect of this is that a significant percentage of the millions of people who need the services of a competent estate liquidator might not ever find one, and they will thereby be at the mercy of secondary and far less optimal market choices, such as garage sales or listing sites like Craigslist or eBay. So, the estate sales business, though large, needs to grow up.

If you have never heard of estate liquidation or have never been to one of the literally thousands of estate sales that happen each month, then you are missing out on one of the most dynamic and effective ways to sell your personal property, and one of the most budget conscious ways to acquire either common household goods or even antiques and collectibles.

The largest estate liquidation companies run their businesses as profession-

The author talks with a customer at an estate sale.

From making arrangements to sell your best, and seeing to the staging of in-house estate sales, estate liquidators are emerging as viable alternatives to auctioneers.

ally as the better auction houses do. They are covered by property and liability insurance, and each of their employees are covered by workers compensation. Also, in states where they are required to do so, they collect sales tax on all sales, which adds to their state's revenues. Many estate liquidators have gross revenues in excess of a million dollars. That is a ton of personal property that gets sold on behalf of their clients every year. Estate sales are not only a vibrate part of the overall economy, they also, because of the sheer diversity of the personal property that gets sold at them, help to economically sustain many niche dealer communities who prefer to shop at them.

••

The reality check these people got is that we, as a consuming society, have a lot of stuff in our homes and when the time comes to empty them, most of us are woefully unprepared.

••

There is not an antiques dealer or a vintage or collectibles eBay seller who has not gone to an estate sale. Collectors and pickers know all about estate sales, and because they can more often than not find unique items there, they carefully plan their weekends, so as to allow them the time flexibility they need in order to shop at them.

Attending an estate sale is one of the two best ways for those in the antiques and collectibles trade to procure their inventories; the other one is auctions. But still there is not a week that goes by that I do not hear from someone who expresses that there was a time in the recent past when they really could have been helped by knowing about an estate liquidator.

Here's the positive side: the word is getting out. The internet is a big factor here and a website is now the single best way for an estate liquidator to let others know about their services. Many companies have even gone the extra mile and set up email notification systems to let their customers know about their upcoming sales. So many estate sales companies have now created websites, that today in the U.S., especially if you live in one of its twenty most populated cities, you can easily find an estate liquidator who is honest, ethical, and highly skilled. .

You just need to know how to look for them, which search terms you'll need to use, and, when you do eventually find an estate sales company in your area, which questions are the best ones to ask in order to learn if they conduct themselves as professionals. By visiting their sites, you can also find out a great deal about their companies estate sales strategies.

I wrote this book for the "little old ladies and men" and their families, for all the people who find themselves in the quandary of what to do with too

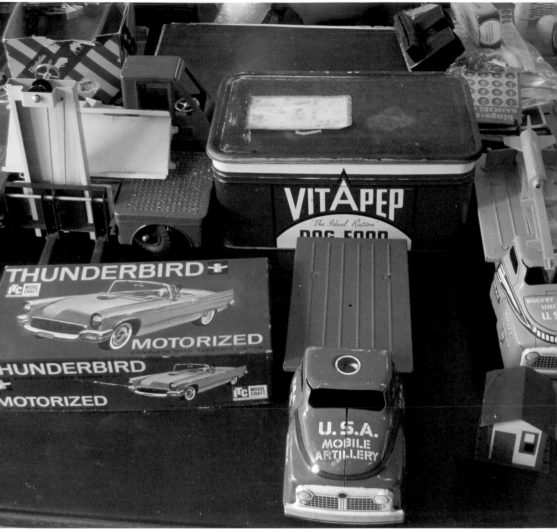

Condition determines value, but don't let a little bit of chipped paint or rust deter you from offering items like these for sale.

much stuff, and all who are overwhelmed by the circumstances that death, relocation, or divorce brings, or by the necessity to take immediate action and sell their personal property.

It is often with a profound sense of doom or feelings of abject despair that people approach the situation of what to do with stuff, and who can really blame them? It is hard to manage the disposition of an entire lifetime of your own or a loved one's accumulations.

It is said that the emotional impact that comes from a death in the family, the loss of a job, or a divorce figure prominently among life's prime stressors. In fact, these life challenges are so demanding and trying to go through, that each of them can be found on most psychology experts' top twenty list of most stressful situations a human can go through. And to this mix, you are adding the hard job of moving an entire household worth of furnishings. That's difficult enough all by itself. So, if the task ahead of you seems depressing and difficult, give yourself a gentle reminder: you are not just dealing with one of life's prime stressors, but also having to figure out how to empty a house of its accumulations in a way that is satisfactory to you and/or the estate you represent

A few of the most consistent statements I hear over and over again from my clients are:

"After what I have gone through with liquidating the personal property of my mother or father, I want to go home and get rid of everything."

"Now I want to be a minimalist."

"Who needs all this crap?"

"Do you think this was the house of a hoarder?"

The reality check these people got is that we, as a consuming society, have a lot of stuff in our homes and when the time comes to empty them, most of us are woefully unprepared.

• •

If you have never heard of estate liquidation or have never been to an estate sale, then you are missing out on one of the most dynamic and effective ways to sell your personal property ...

• •

Most people don't think they are as hungry for stuff or the acquisition of things as others; they feel they have their gathering instinct under control. But take a look at your home. Most of you are fairly neat and tidy, and proud of the comfort and order that you have created where you live. So, you can't fathom how someone else can let it get so bad. But if you were to take everything out of every drawer, box or cupboard in your home and lay it all out and let a stranger look at it, they might think your home had the appearance of a hoarder's house.

Our homes are filled with a wild assortment of things. Closets, basements, attics and garages are often deeply layered in sedimentary fashion, and often you can figure out the time line of the items stored in these areas by the depth at which you find them.

Most of us are like this. We have clothes we never wear hanging in multiple closets, and carefully wrapped items in boxes in our garages that for some reason we can't part with. Our kitchen cupboards are stacked high with mugs, incomplete sets of dishes, and chipped or cracked serving sets. We are storing pans without lids, and gadgets we'll never use in our kitchen's every nook and cranny. Let's not even go into what you may have stored in your attics and basements, or what you pay on a monthly basis to store your stuff in a public storage unit. Let's just admit it: all of us have a ton of stuff.

For the most part, the solutions to the problem of what to do with everything that this book will help you with are mostly about how to help you organize and sell someone else's stuff. But you will also be able to use this book to reach your goals if you are recently divorced or otherwise downsizing.

No one wants to make mistakes about how much something is worth. Is it a treasure you've found in the attic, or a tiddly wink trinket not worth a dollar? This is not an easy question to answer. To do it right and bring in the most income for your precious cargo takes years of experience, and even then it is a daunting task.

I have spent the last seventeen years conducting in-house public estate sales in the San Francisco Bay area. The biggest lesson I have learned in all those years is how little I know and how much I have yet to learn. I admit this to you as a person who has sold $250,000 paintings, coin collections worth as much as $350,000, and a single silver dagger for over $90,000.

....

The way to add value to an estate is to add time.
The way to irreversibly deduct value from an estate is
to take away time by acting with haste.

....

I've had great success in this business and because my intelligence and character get tested each and every day, I have become all the more acute when it comes to my knowledge, and all the more ethical when it comes to staying honest, even when I find $10,000 in cash in a drawer that no one, and I do mean no one, would ever know about. So, it's not that I don't know a great deal, it's that there is a great deal to know.

The fact of how much there is to know, and the impossibility of any one person knowing it all, even so called professionals, means that you, gentle reader, don't stand a chance unless you learn how to ask the right people the right questions, and form a comprehensive action plan from their answers.

The way to add value to an estate is to add time, so give yourself some. The way to irreversibly deduct value from an estate is to take away time by acting with haste.

Study the information contained in this book. Talk to your friends and rela-

Items like this beautifully carved and painted leather book slip case cover will find ready buyers at an estate sale.

tives and get their opinions. Ask your family, realtors, and attorneys about the mistakes and success they've heard about others making when they were faced with your kind of situations. Learn from the experiences, either positive or negative, that others who have gone before you have had.

Chapter 1

....

ESTATE SALES:

The Billion Dollar Business You May Never Have Heard Of

EACH WEEK, ONE OF THE WORLD'S MAJOR AUCTION HOUSES announces to the press that they have just sold a miracle treasure for something like a bazillion dollars. Items so rare and wonderful, that collectors the world over beat a path to their doors with buckets of cash, which they then spent, thereby setting outrageous world records for the most amount of money ever spent on whatever ... and we are awed by this, as we should be.

Here's the important thing people reading these stories don't realize: Most of the time, these record-breaking results are for items that came out of someone's house. Yes, sometimes those "houses" are staggeringly palatial and grand in scope, but not always. Sometimes the most interesting and valuable items sold at auction come from small town, white-picket-fence homes, or from inner-city apartments. All my years in the estate liquidation business continue to teach me over and over again that there is solid truth in the old prospectors' saying, "Gold? Gold is where you find it."

Take the case of the astonished man who, while watching an episode of *Antiques Roadshow*, saw one of the show's appraisers look over an old blanket and declare to the shocked person who brought it in that it was one of the finest examples of a first phase Navajo chief's blanket he had ever seen, and worth hundreds of thousands of dollars.

• •

Each and every week, one of the world's major auction houses announces to the press that they have just sold a miracle treasure for something like a bazillion dollars. Sometimes the most interesting and valuable items sold at auction come from small town, white picket fence homes or inner city apartments.

• •

What astonished the man watching the show was that he was pretty sure he had a blanket that was exactly like it. It had been in his family since the 1870s. It was just hanging around his house somewhere. Not one of his family members for the many years that they had owned this blanket ever imagined that it might be rare and wonderful. And here was someone on TV now saying it was worth an incredible sum. Whoa!

SOLD FOR:
More than $1 million

This Navajo First Phase Chief's blanket was sold by John Moran Auctioneers for $1.8 million on June 19, 2012.

John Moran Auctioneers

SOLD FOR:
More than $2.22 million

There are still treasures to be discovered either in your own home or someone else's. This 1,000-year-old Chinese "Ding" bowl from the Northern Song Dynasty, scooped up at a yard sale for no more than $3, was sold at Sotheby's Auction House in March 2013 for more than $2.22 million. *Sotheby's*

So, sometime before June 2012, the man walked into John Moran Auctioneers in Southern California on a free appraisal clinic day, and laid before the amazed appraisers a first phase Navajo chief's blanket that turned out to be even better than the one on *Antiques Roadshow*. After careful analysis and the use of outside appraisers, John Moran Auctioneers established an auction estimate, which this chief's blanket blew through and beyond, and it sold for the princely sum of $1.8 million on June 19, 2012.

Please get my point! Great stuff can come out of an average home, and maybe even your home. The discovery and sale of an item of great worth has life-changing consequences for all the members of a family. Be careful and diligent with your stuff.

It is a reality that many of the glittering and prized objects you routinely see published in auction house catalogs were consigned to those auction houses by executors and estate representatives i.e., just plain folks. Any regular person can find gold and it happens every day.

LET'S BACK UP A BIT

What do I mean by the title of this chapter? Of course, most of you have heard of, or have interacted with, aspects of the estate sales industry, but what I am asking you to do here, because one day you will need to know this, is to see how all of this industry's many parts fit together and are part of a comprehensible whole. You can understand this, if you take a look at and study its many parts, one by one.

When the popular *Antiques Roadshow* comes on TV each week showing an expert describing an item and appraising it as something that has great worth, you're hooked. You want to be that person standing there with the crooked smile saying, "Me? I have a treasure? Well blimey." You are captivated. When those crazy *Storage Wars*' guys bid higher and higher amounts for a storage locker containing who knows what, you think they're nuts. But are they nuts or savvy-minded business people looking to make big scores? Folks, they are not nuts—they are in the know. Their business model is predicated on the fact that people will make mistakes and leave valuable stuff behind; that's how the *Storage Wars*' guys make their living.

· ·

If you are not discovering that your stuff has value, or are enjoying the income from its sale, then someone savvier will be the one to enjoy the benefits. Diligence is key.

· ·

Auction houses all across America, from the small mom and pops to the large international ones, are primarily stocked with the personal property that comes out of millions of homes around the world and was once someone's personal property. And then, owned for some period of time by someone else, it eventually finds its way back into the marketplace and is bought again. It's part of the life cycle of stuff: to be bought, used, and sold again. If you are not the one discovering that your stuff has value, or are enjoying the income from its sale, then someone savvier will be the one to enjoy the benefits. Diligence is the key.

Antiques stores sell old stuff. And you, because you like very old stuff, have shopped them for years seeking furnishings, paintings, porcelains, or whatever other kind of antiques and collectibles you fancy. Where do you think the antiques dealers get all that old stuff? It doesn't just appear in their stores looking chic. Antiques dealers go to estate sales and auctions and most of what they have came out of someone's estate. You have more power than you think. You and the estate you represent are primary inventory providers for anyone in the buy-and-sell game. Your estate's stuff is what helps to keep a large industry healthy and strong. Never forget that you are an important player.

The most popular series on PBS television is the *Antiques Roadshow*, where each week people bring items in for experts to look over, hoping that they will turn out to be rare and valuable. Everyone wants to hear the expert exclaim, "Oh my, what you have here is a treasure." The items people bring to the show fall into one of two broad categories: either they were family heirlooms or things they had the great good fortune to find and buy for a song at an antiques store, auction, or estate sale.

Every single day of the year, tens of thousands of people who are in charge of what to do with an estate's personal property are trying to figure out if they or their family should retain items from an estate, sell, donate, or throw stuff away. These are the people who are executors, heirs, fiduciaries, and attorneys. It is their obligation to maximize the value of the estates they represent. If they take the time and educate themselves, they'll have a good chance of fulfilling this duty. If they are lax or lazy or even because they are overwhelmed, and they don't educate themselves, they will give away the farm.

. . . .

Every day of the year, tens of thousands of people who are in charge of what to do with an estate's personal property are trying to figure out if they or their family should retain items from an estate, sell, donate, or throw stuff away.

. . . .

What about you? How prepared are you? How much are you willing to learn about the how of "how to sell stuff?" Do you want to be the smiling person on *Antiques Roadshow* getting all the attention or do you want to be the person stewing on a couch at home, watching when someone else brings an item up that you sold them for way too cheap and listen as they are told what the item really is, and how it's worth the price of a small tropical island?

You need to know how much an item is worth in order to make your best selling decisions. Many will either never figure it out, or will only partially figure it out, because who you need to turn to and get assistance from is just under the radar screen of you perception. Many of you have not yet seen or discovered that there is an entire group of professionals who can aid and assist you with their unique skills and give you all the information you need.

These professionals are auctioneers, estate liquidators, antiques dealers, senior move specialists, professional organizers, and pickers. Each of these types of professionals represents an integral part of the overall, and staggeringly large, business of seeing to the needs of people and their families who want to sell their stuff. That you do not yet comprehend how each of these

Some of these antique dog show medals are sterling and the box of them has a value of $1,000.

There are at least 19 different Hummel maker's marks. The one on yours will determine its value.

professionals fits into the jigsaw puzzle of the whole is understandable. This subject is vast.

For a while, you are going to feel like a jockey racing around and around the track of options. It is going to seem like there are too many competing ideas about what you should do with your family's personal property. Confusion at this point is the norm. Take time to learn about the specific services that each of these types of professionals provide. Read this book and others like it. In a short while, you will begin to understand the differences that define the services of each of these professionals. And then you will be better able to choose one or more of them to help you through the process.

Your stuff, when sold, and added to the stuff that is sold by hundreds of thousands of families a year at auction, amounts to billions of dollars. The combined yearly income statistics for just the world's two largest auction houses, Sotheby's and Christie's, is over ten billion dollars. You are part of this—a small part, but a part nonetheless. When you add the income that gets generated on a yearly basis from the thousands of auction houses across America to the income from all the in-house estate sales that occur every week in this country, the total yearly income for the sale of personal property in America boggles the mind. It is truly astonishing.

SO WHAT. WHO NEEDS TO KNOW ABOUT THIS, ANYWAY?

You do!

Last year, approximately two million people passed away in America, and all of them had stuff. Every year, a tsunami-sized wave of personal property has to be dealt with; this is sad, of course, but what's sadder to me is how so much of this personal property finds its way into landfills, is purchased for pennies on the dollar by unscrupulous dealers, or gets placed into storage for years and becomes of no use to anyone because of neglect and the ravages of time.

I will not write about this in the abstract, though. Every one of the two million people or so who pass away each year in America represents a human life. They're our family members, part of our community of friends, or in some other way are people we cared about and respected.

Their stuff matters in 100 different ways and your most important way to relate to it is not to feel that you have been burdened or given an insurmountable task by them, but to honor their wishes in relationship to their stuff in the same way you would wish to be honored about the various choices you might make about your own. The second most important way for you, your family, or this person's closest friends to consider when approaching a decedent's personal property, is to make sure that each of you retain something of true sentimental value from their effects.

Some of these people were incredibly adept at gathering and amassing their collections, their homes looking like museums or art galleries—each taking care to the documentation and preservation of their collections—while others of more modest means or more practical natures filled their homes with just enough utilitarian objects and furnishings to make their homes or dwellings comfortable places to live in.

The one thing these two groups of people most definitely have in common is that on passing, their families or loved ones will have to figure out what to do with their worldly possessions. That is why I wrote this book.

IN THE PAST

The way that people in the recent past dealt with the personal property of someone who had just passed away was to retain some of it by virtue of inheritance, and then whatever they didn't want or need would be sent to one of the local auction houses.

If it was really fancy stuff that needed to be sold, those items were sent to big city auction houses, and if what they had wasn't so fancy, or even if it was downright modest or had little value, those items would get sent to one of the local small town rural or regional auction houses. In this way, families effectively were able to deal with the sale of their loved one's personal property and to empty houses, making them ready for sale.

The way our grandmothers and grandfathers handled the personal property of the estates they had to deal with was to keep some of it and give the rest of it away. It was all so simple because few people knew what the true value of things were, or even how to reach out to someone who might.

We are much more of a researching type of society today. We look things up. We expect to find professionals to aid and assist us through any number of issues or problems we may have. And we don't want to be the person in the story who was taken advantage of, who had a family treasure robbed from them, who was duped, or misinformed. It isn't going to be easy, this circumstance you find yourself in, and you really won't be able to do it all yourself. You're going to need to find people you can rely upon.

SOLD FOR:
$500

This four-piece Russian silver set with Kiddush cup, circa 1878, sold at an estate sale for $500.

SOLD FOR:
$200

Schaubach Kunst nude on a rearing horse sold at an estate sale for $200.

The right professionals working for you will add income far in excess of any fee they may charge. Pay their fees, and enjoy the additional income their services bring.

WELCOME TO THE SECRET WORLD OF STUFF

When a family member or loved one passes away, most people will have to take a crash course in what to do with all of their stuff. It won't be as easy as it was in your grandmother's or grandfather's day. It's not only the stuff you'll have to deal with, of course; there's also the lawyers for legal matters, realtors for selling the house, contractors to fix whatever is broken, antiques dealers to call for opinions, auctioneers to generate appraisals, and estate liquidators—and each of them will have a language and jargon all their own, which will not always be easy to understand.

No one has been pre-trained in the science of what to do with stuff. We're not born with this knowledge, it's not taught in schools, and there are few books on the subject; for the most part, only people who have to deal with stuff every day really know how to deal with it, and even for them it's no cakewalk. And you have never had to walk into your mom's or dad's house with the intended purpose of opening up all their drawers and rifling through their closets. But now you're going to have to do that. You're going to learn more than you ever wanted to know about your parents and loved ones, and you are going to learn some of their secrets and will have to find a way to hold those secrets honorably. It's been like a law to you that you were never to explore the parts of their lives that were sensitive and private, but with their passing, that has been changed by the necessity of having to now take certain actions. Try to remember that this is an unfolding process that will get easier, especially if you combine the task with a sense of respect and accord your loved ones with a right to their humanness. We all have secrets in our drawers, and your parents and other loved ones are certainly no different.

ESTATE SALES ARE A BILLION DOLLAR PART OF THE ESTATE LIQUIDATION INDUSTRY

Rain predicted? It's going to be a blistering hot summer day? Your weatherman is promising snow levels up to your eyeballs? None of that will matter, if it's the weekend. Friday, Saturday, and Sunday are prime estate sale shopping days, and people who shop at them will not be deterred from their agendas by the weather. They must go because none of them wants to miss what could be an exciting and profitable foray into the environs of a stranger's home.

A simple drive through any city this weekend will prove how popular estate sales are. As you drive around, look for estate sale directional signs taped to utility poles, or for the printed sandwich board signs that are put up by professional estate sales companies. To see firsthand how all this works, get to the estate on the first day of the sale and several hours before it opens. What you'll see when you get there will be a long line of shoppers. Some of these shoppers will have been there since the wee morning hours, not wanting to lose their place in line.

Chats about having an estate sale or going to one and letting other people know what you find are all over social media sites like Facebook and Twitter. Estate sales are a true buying and shopping phenomena for millions of people. Dealers and collectors of every stripe have added the practice of shopping at estate sales to their weekly inventory acquisition trips, faithfully going to them in addition to the flea markets and local auctions they used to only go to.

Forget *American Pickers*, take your eyes off the latest *Storage Wars* episode, and even though *Pawn Stars* segments are so compelling and interesting, take a moment and realize that there in your own town or city, hundreds of thousands, or maybe even millions, of dollars worth of personal property is being bought and sold on a regular basis. But it's almost like it's all being done in secret.

IS IGNORANCE BLISS?

Because you did not need to know what to do with personal property until someone passed away, you never learned about the auction, antiques, or estate sales businesses. But to stay ignorant at this point, now that you and your family need this information, will cost you money. So, ask yourself how much money you are willing to give up to stay uninformed. Each week in hundreds of towns and cities, regular folks are being "picked" by dealers and unwittingly giving away millions of dollars worth of their families' personal property to the eager strangers they have invited into their homes.

WHAT IT MEANS TO BE PICKED

To do things all by yourself is to agree to stay ignorant about the fact that there are a great many respectable and professional individuals working in the antiques, auction, and estate sales business, whose many talents are available to you right now. Being picked mostly happens to people because they either don't want to take the time to learn what an item is and what its potential value might be, or they don't know how to do that.

Once jewelry has been appraised, an estate sale is an excellent place to sell it to the public.

Here is an example: Someone who doesn't know better decides to sell his or her items to a dealer who has published a want list in a local newspaper. What the potential seller is responding to is the flashy two-page photo spread of items the dealer says they want to buy. The person who doesn't know any better looks over the list and notices several items they have recently inherited. Right next to the item description will be the published amount the dealer states they're willing to pay. The potential seller gets all excited, packs up the items they want to sell, and races down to meet the dealer, who has set up in some hotel conference room downtown.

They meekly present the item and are crestfallen to hear the dealer's offer, but not so crestfallen that they don't sell the item. After all, the dealer had patiently explained to them all the nuanced ways their item was not exactly the same, and therefore was not as valuable as the item that they published in the newspaper. But they're willing to take it off the seller's hands, and so the seller agrees to the sum offered, which was less than was published, and then goes home.

Later the seller becomes concerned enough about the whole transaction to finally look the item up, only to discover that they got about 10 cents on the dollar. They've been picked.

USE A PROFESSIONAL SERVICE OR GET PICKED

This is the overriding theme of this book: if you choose to ignore the excellent services of professionals who are available to you, or you choose to try and navigate your way through all the many complications that selling stuff will present to you by yourself, you will get picked.

Most families who stage their own estate sales, sell individual items to antiques dealers, take the family's gold and silver to a scrap dealer, or who won't send their property to the right auction house, will get picked. These families or their representatives don't fully comprehend that by using the wrong sales approach, the estates they represent will experience income losses of 50 to 70 percent of the total value of the estate, possibly even more.

They don't get that by doing it themselves, they are unwittingly and collectively giving away untold thousands of dollars. The crazy thing about this is how much of their decision to do it themselves is not just about wanting to take the easy way out because of time constraints or confusion, but also they think that doing it themselves will save their estates lots of money. The right professionals working for you will add income far in excess of any fee they may charge. Pay their fees, and enjoy the additional income their services bring.

SOLD FOR:
$1,200

This pre-Columbian figure sold at auction for $1,200.

ANOTHER PART OF THE SECRET

Because so many of them have justifiable fears of competition, estate liquidators, antiques dealers, and auctioneers maintain far too much secrecy and non-transparency about their business practices. They have not allowed themselves the benefits that would come to them were they to reveal to as many people as possible the nature of their buying and selling strategies. Transparency is a good thing. People like to know what is going on. They want to know what all of their options are. They want to deal with professionals who are not afraid to direct them to the services of their competition if it would be in the best interest of the client.

If you do this right and connect to the right people and make sure you ask the right questions, you'll have a much better chance of experiencing the big positive surprise.

Because of the desire for revenue, you will sometimes see a small auction house attempt to sell a rare and valuable antique. This is not a scenario that will work out financially for their client, but it will bring income into the small auction house. When a small auction house does something like that, their actions can only be viewed as being self-serving. They don't know yet how to serve your estate's better interest by referring your business elsewhere and still make money. The only place to sell a wonderfully rare and expensive item is to send it to one of the big auction houses, but you might not ever know this unless someone tells you. And the small auction houses might not tell you to send it to a bigger auction house because they do not want to lose the revenue. These segments of the estate liquidation industry, because they are so hesitant to share information and business with each other, have created, by this lack of sharing, the unintended consequence of causing and sustaining consumer ignorance. You are going to have to get comfortable asking the so-called experts a lot of questions about issues like these.

Part of the problem, at least from the standpoint of the in-house, public estate sales business, is that, as an industry, estate liquidators have never properly composed themselves into even one nationally recognized association. Almost no state in the United States regulates its activities, and there are no recognized national certification programs that will either teach or train people how to best stage and conduct an estate sales business. How then are consumers supposed to know what to do, where to turn, and what the industry's best practices are when it comes to having an estate sale in their home?

They, at least for the time being, are left to their own skills at gathering and deciphering information.

And even though antiques dealers own stores or have space in antiques malls and collectives or are members of national antiques dealers associations, their individual buying practices really follow no standards. None of them publishes their buying practices. There won't be a chart in their stores explaining in any detail what their offers for your stuff is based on. Are they buying your stuff for half price and doubling their money, or are they buying your item for ten cents on the dollar? You won't know unless you ask, so I encourage you to ask. In general, what they'll offer you for an item is only vaguely in relationship to what the item is worth, and their offers will too often depend on how much money they have available for buying, or their perceptions of how little you might be willing to accept.

THE IN-HOUSE ESTATE SALES BUSINESS

According to estatesales.net, there are over 2,000 estate liquidators in America that regularly list on the site. These companies account for as many as 4,000 estate sales each month. That's 48,000 estate sales a year. There are other estate liquidators as well who choose to list their sales on two other sites, estatesales.org and estatesales.com. Then there are hundreds of estate sales companies that don't list on these three sites, choosing instead to rely on their own websites or Craigslist, or both to list their sales.

Based upon the information I could get from estatesale.net and extrapolating a bit, I propose that in America each month, about 8,000 professionally conducted estate sales are held. That's 96,000 a year.

So, if every estate sale that a professional stages somewhere in America on a yearly basis were to average $10,000 in sales, and if my extrapolation of the incomplete data from the three websites is correct, then on a yearly basis, $960 million worth of personal property is sold out of people's homes. That's a boatload of cash that gets generated from the sale of simple pots and pans, couches and chairs, entire truckloads of dishes, cars, and paintings. In short, this income is generated from the sale of anything you might find in a house. This income comes from homes just like the one you are faced with having to liquidate. Like it or not, your estate is part of this huge marketplace.

STUFF CREATES BIG BUCKS: AS IN BILLIONS!

Don't get left out. Realize that there's big bucks in stuff and ask lots of people lots of questions about their experiences dealing with the personal property from an estate they have had to take care of. Learn from others. Follow the advice of competent professionals. Check out people's references. Interview more than one professional. Remember that confusion, and I know

The sale of simple household items, like regular dishes and fine china, can add up to a lot of cash. These are two different Lenox China patterns worth about $225 to $300 each.

this gets a little hard to believe, is a state of learning. Make sure you get your slice, even if it's a small one, of the big billion-dollar estate sales pie. Your family and the estate you have inherited deserve this.

You're going to be okay. It doesn't matter that auctioneers, estate sales professionals, antiques dealers, and pickers are doing whatever they are doing, good or bad, while they conduct business in their own individual ways. Some of these professionals will be sharks or charlatans, and some will be more like saints or scholars. Your number one preoccupation should be arming yourself with as much high quality information as you can gather in order to best protect yourself.

....

This circumstance you find yourself in isn't going to be easy, and you really won't be able to do it all yourself. You're going to need to find people you can rely upon.

....

It's like one of the first lessons you had to learn as a child: It's a great big world out there, full of the unexpected. Remember there are two sides of the unexpected: one we might as well call the big positive surprise, and one the big negative surprise.

If you do this right and connect to the right people and make sure you ask the right questions, you'll have a much better chance of experiencing the big positive surprise. But if you are not going to participate in the process and take care of yourself, can you really expect that anyone else will? See yourself as a partner and as a co-creator of your estate's best possible outcome. It's not a given that you will be taken advantage of, unless you abdicate or shirk your responsibilities.

Get used to living outside of your comfort zones and take charge. You will be dealing with perfect strangers, so this is where good common sense, instincts, and consulting with other family members comes in. You are going to need many resources in order to make sense out of what people are telling you, and to understand whether they are telling the truth or trying to take advantage of you. There is simply no easy way around the requirement that to get great results, you will need to put great effort into the task. Look for people with verifiable track records or who were referred to you by friends and family members.

The most common mistake a person in your position can make is to give up before trying, and blaming others for the hardship of it all. But mistakes like giving up or blaming others will only lead to someone else pocketing your family's fortunes and leave you to wonder how you might have done any of it differently.

Chapter 2

THE BLOOD, SWEAT AND TEARS OF STUFF

I WISH THAT THERE WAS a way that I could wave a magic wand, get you to turn three times, and have you click your heels together ala Dorothy in *The Wizard of Oz*—asking you in my calmest voice to open your eyes and see that the house you were tasked with emptying is, in fact, empty, but for the love you felt there.

But that would be a fantasy less believable than the looking glass that Alice found herself slipping through. The big emptying-the-house project you are facing now won't get itself done by the dint of fantasy or daydreams. There will be no genie coming with minions, no dwarves arriving to shoulder your burdens singing "Hi Ho Hi Ho." Your task, your responsibility, the hard work that you are about to undertake on behalf of an estate, is not a dream. It's real, and it will take much new learning on your part to get through the process successfully.

There must be a hundred ways to empty out a house of its decades worth of personal property, but none of them will be easy. Stuff is sticky. Your mom loved it or your dad bought it during a once-in-a-lifetime trip to Europe as a young man. Your parents, or maybe it was your kindly aunt or respectable uncle, told you so many stories about the items in their homes, and yes, they sometimes warned you in low stage whispers to be careful with their stuff, that this or that item had great value. Because of your love and loyalty, and caring for them, you agreed to help. Many of you will wish in the coming days that you had not been so quick to agree.

· ·

If it gets contentious between you and anyone else who is named in the will, do not be surprised when any one player uses the personal property as a weapon.

· ·

You promised, maybe even at or close to the time of their deaths, to protect them by taking care of their stuff—to make sure that the contents of their homes would be distributed correctly to other family members, and then that you would sell or donate the rest of their worldly possessions in some way to their best advantage.

When it comes time to empty out a house and you see a mess like this, you may feel stressed and want to give up, and that's a normal reaction. But hang in there. While the task will be hard, it's not impossible and you will get through it.

Of course, when you made that promise, you really didn't know what you were promising, how hard the task might be, or just how much time this effort on their behalf would take away from your own pressing problems. Going through another person's home, making the thousands of little decisions about what to do with all of the stuff those houses contain turns out to be difficult; it's not long before you grasp that while there are solutions to these sorts of problems, most of those solutions come with complications all their own.

We all have our own personal lives to consider, don't we? Who's got the time to manage the affairs of someone else? Most of us are stressed already by a multitude of tasks we need to accomplish for ourselves every day. But a promise is a promise, so we dutifully proceed.

In order to equitably divide an estate's silver, you also need to be able to tell the difference between sterling and silver plate, which is all in how they are marked.

THE EMOTIONAL SIDE OF STUFF

When I stated earlier that stuff is sticky, I mean that stuff, especially a loved one's stuff, can get connected by us or by others to the person who once owned it and has recently passed away. In the extreme, to some, stuff takes on a semi-spiritual or even mystical quality. If you hurt the stuff, throw the wrong stuff away, or give an object to the wrong person, there are some who may become afraid that the deceased will come back to haunt them. I am not kidding about this being some people's reaction.

But maybe you're not the way-over-the-top type—you have a good head on a strong set of shoulders and mystical thoughts like those are way too esoteric for you. Your feet are squarely on the ground about all of this. You're intelligent, reasonable, and rational—you know that stuff is just stuff, and you have decided that you are going to approach the whole process of sorting through stuff logically. This will only work if you are an only child or the sole person who is inheriting the stuff, because, and this is almost always true, everybody else who is connected to inheriting the stuff will most definitely have an opinion about what the stuff is, and what course of action is best to deal with it. Opinions from the family about the stuff are going to be voiced, emails are going to get written, there may be debates around the dinner table ... people may get heated about all of this. Some will stubbornly insist contrary to your own sense of logic, or even counter to the will of the deceased, that certain things need to happen. Get ready to meet your family again.

• •

Some will stubbornly insist contrary to your own sense of logic, or even counter to the will of the deceased, that certain things need to happen. Get ready to meet your family again.

• •

Your family is going to show up just exactly as they have always showed up, as themselves. If in the past you have had trouble communicating with any one of your family members or their spouses, you're still going to have trouble with them. Both of you are still going to try to prove the point of whatever you have been trying to for years. That's just the way it is. If it is a creepy friend of the deceased who is now in the mix because they have been left some aspect of the decedent's personal property, they are still going to appear creepy to you. Everyone is going to be themselves.

If it gets contentious between you and anyone else who is named in the will, do not be surprised when any one player uses the personal property as a weapon. They will do this. "You didn't love dad; if you did, you wouldn't get

Have dad tell you who should get his pipes and watches.

Likewise, have mom say who gets her collection of carnival glass and other glassware.

rid of his chair." "You want to sell mom's jewelry? How dare you; if you loved her, if you cared a measly thing about her, you would give it to me, her favorite daughter." The harangue coming from those who aggressively disagree with you will be super creative, pull no punches, and seem endlessly repetitive. Even family members who you thought could be counted on to take your side may interfere. This is all normal and people just being people.

Short of expensive family therapy sessions, tightly packing into Sunday church pews and praying together, or a sudden thunder crack of good old fashion divine intervention that gets the family to sort the whole estate mess out, you could propose something radical. You could ask everyone to remember what the decedent said over the course of years about what they wanted to have happen to their stuff, and combine that with a careful reading and following of their last will and testament. It's still their stuff, folks, and will be until it has been distributed according to their wishes. The stuff they left is a gift, not an entitlement.

MEET THE DECEDENT

Who was the decedent and what did they really want?

At the end of the day, it doesn't really matter what you or any other family members want to have happen to the stuff. If there is a will, the only thing that matters is what the decedent wanted.

Of course, it's easier if there is a will that spells out what you as an executor or trustee are suppose to do with every last thing the decedent owned. The trouble is, no one leaves a will like that. People have wills drawn up detailing what should happen with what they think are the important things in their estate. So, their will may describe what to do with a hundred or so things that are in the house or in a safety deposit box somewhere and you, as the executor, will be left to decide what to do with the rest.

As hard as that sort of will is to interpret, at least it has some specific instructions. How about when their instructions are general or vague about a few categories of things and absolutely nonspecific about everything else? "My daughter gets the jewelry and my sons get the guns." Or what do you do with the stuff when everyone gets an equal share? "I leave all the contents of my home to my four children." What are you supposed to do with that sort of instruction? That's when disputes may start, when the dander gets raised or worse, when lines get drawn and sides chosen.

• •

The stuff the decedent left is a gift, not an entitlement.

• •

Here is when you have to go back to the beginning, at least symbolically, to what you know about the decedent and do some interpretation. Did they ever mention to you in conversation what their wishes were? Did they ever point to an item and say that they wanted it to go to a specific person? Did they talk about donating things not named in their will to a charity instead of giving it to the family? Also, some people leave little notes attached to the things in their home that state this goes to so and so, and this vase, I want my nieces to have it.

It is a difficult predicament to have to interpret what someone might have wanted done with their personal property when there is not much in the way of any actual instructions they've left to give you guidance. Consider asking your attorney for their opinion. If there is little debate or disputes between family members, and they all seem reasonable, you could call a family meeting to help decide what to do. If they are all fighting, you are going to need to have a meeting anyway, but before you do, develop a plan and prepare yourself in all the ways that you can because a meeting like that is difficult, trying, and draining. Take care of yourself.

If all else fails, use a lottery system or draw straws or numbers out of a hat to establish an order by which things from the house can be chosen. Don't laugh. I have seen this work many a time. It is hard to argue with the idea of random. No one chose sides. No one played favorites. It was numbers pulled out of a hat or short or long straws that decided, the fates, as it were, that did the choosing.

The letter below is an example of how you might approach your parents while they're still alive about what their wishes are concerning the handing down of their personal property.

A LETTER ABOUT STUFF

Dear Mom or Dad,

You have already given me the greatest gift that anyone could ever give, and that is the gift of life. I thank you for this. Also, it has been through our many interactions and conversations that you have graced me with your experience and wisdom, and from that I have learned much.

Our experiences of interacting together have ranged all over the map. We have been good and bad to each other. We have enriched each other. We have hurt each other. And above all else, we have loved each other. Family love, even in the hardest of times, has been the resilient stitch that has woven and kept us together.

You are getting older now. I do not know how many more Thanksgiving and Christmas dinners we might share, how many more letters we might write, or phone calls we might make to each other late at night talking about whatever. I only know that we have less time than we once did. So while we still have time to talk about such things, I would like to suggest that we talk about what you want to have happen with your stuff—the things that you have acquired or inherited over the course of your lifetime.

You are the best person to decide what to do with your stuff. Who knows what you want to have happen to your accumulations better than you? It's not your family's stuff yet and won't be until you decide that it is.

Sometimes even in families where everyone gets along, arguments and disagreements can arise about the small stuff in an estate when there are no specific instructions about what to do with those kinds of items; who should get what, and how. I know that you have already written a will and it outlines your instructions concerning the property of your estate, so it will be easy for all concerned to understand exactly what your wishes are in relationship

As you search through your parents' belongings, you may find secret letters and photos. Tend to these with the same respect you would ask of others about your secrets.

to what you have explicitly dictated. We all thank you for that. It's the little things, though, that are not described in the will. Because you owned them, it may become so important to one or more of your family members about what to do with those things that arguments may arise.

Perhaps a good idea for you would be to call together a family meeting and let us know what your wishes are concerning the many small things in your home. This would give everybody a chance to hear directly from you what you would like to have done. It also would give you the opportunity to hear from others, and what is important to them. What each of your family members has to say concerning the objects in your home may surprise you. People relate to the stuff of others in ways that are interesting. A meeting like this could reveal your family's relationship to the memory of you and your stuff, like how your watch reminds someone of a specific interaction that the two of you had, a conversation maybe. Or how a set of silver reminds someone about some past, glorious grand holiday dinner, when a special milestone was announced to all who were gathered there.

But maybe you do not share my concerns. Maybe you wish that I had never broached the subject at all and remained silent—that it really doesn't matter what happens to your stuff; that it's best to let those who are left behind deal with the thousands of little things in your home. Perhaps you're of the opinion that by my bringing this to your attention, I am being disrespectful, but that is not my intention—quite the opposite really. I am asking you to consider these matters precisely as my demonstration of respect. If it is your stance that others can and should be the ones to figure out what you may have wanted done with your stuff without your specific instructions, I can be okay with that. It's your stuff.

I only ask then for one little favor: Tend to your secrets.

We all have secrets, whether small or big. Both kinds are still secrets, though, and by definition, secrets are things we don't want other people and maybe most especially our children to know. No one in your family really wants to find out something about you that you have kept a secret. I'm not saying that you have secrets, only that if you do, that you remove those kinds of items that reveal your secrets from your home as soon as possible.

When you pass, hopefully many years from now, someone is going to have to sort through all of your possessions. They will see everything. They will learn many things that they did not previously know. If you had a secret lover, letters and pictures from them, get rid of them. If once upon a time you collected erotica or still have a vast collection of pornography and you don't want anybody to know about that, get rid of that stuff. If there was bad blood between you and any one of your relatives, details about secret deals, embarrassing or compromising correspondences of any kind, if you do not want us to see that stuff, get rid of it.

If you need help accomplishing the above, please know that there are people out there who can help you. They are called professional organizers. With their aid and assistance, you will be able to properly take care of that portion of your personal property that you do not wish to burden your family with.

With Affection,
Your Son or Daughter

Chapter 3

YOUR MISTAKES WILL MAKE OTHERS LOTS OF MONEY

IT'S A COLD HARD FACT that people who specialize in finding treasures do so all across America today. And, as mentioned in Chapter 1, they find these treasures in homes just like yours. Some of the absolutely fantastic and valuable items that get brought into the auction market each year, items that scale the heights of believability and sell for more dough than their original sellers could ever have imagined, come from little old mom and pop garage sales, estate sales, and small-time auctions.

It's true that some of these outrageous finds can be attributed to weekend warrior garage sale fanatics, shoppers out for a weekend joyride on the estate sales superhighway of stuff. And some of these Good Golly Miss Molly moments of, "I can't believe they found that treasure," are bought by collectors who shop estate sales on a periodic basis. But I am guessing that those who are the most likely to land on the X-marks-the-jackpot spot are people who have come to be known as "pickers."

Pickers have three things you do not: time, money to risk, and knowledge.

They faithfully go out every weekend looking for garage and estate sales. For them, it's like a hunting expedition. If they are patient and lay low, the "buck" will come into their sights and they will pull the trigger. It's nothing for them to search for sales through a town's quiet streets and buying wherever they can before heading out, generally to the edge of the city to spend the rest of the day looking for deals at any of several flea markets.

• •

What is worse than putting too much money in other people's pockets because of your lack of knowledge? Throwing items of value away, which is what a lot of you will be tempted to do.

• •

Time is on the picker's side. They work the averages. If it takes going to a hundred yard or garage sales before they hit pay dirt and make a great score, they don't mind.

Here's how most people, who are sailing into uncharted waters by deciding to do their own estate sale, will make their first mistake and stuff a wad of cash in a picker's pocket: They're going to think that they can outsmart or prepare

If you have a basic knowledge of antiques and collectibles, and a keen eye, you can find little treasures at estate sales, such as this Shawnee clown cookie jar and Hubley cast iron Boston Terrier doorstop.

for a picker's arrival by the simple fact that they have spent a week or two researching the values of their antiques and collectibles on their own. But let me just say, your little week or two spent researching can't compete in any real or significant way with the many years a picker has been consolidating their knowledge base. Taking the time to do research before your sale will help, but without outside expert assistance, you are doomed.

GET HELP

Open up any general price guide about antiques and collectibles, such as *Warman's Antiques and Collectibles Price Guide* and *Antique Trader Antiques and Collectibles Price Guide* by Krause Publications, and look through their hundreds of categories about antiques and collectibles, and as you do, take into consideration that for every single category that these guidebooks detail, there is a picker. So, when you open up your sale, if it contains antiques, collectibles, silver or artwork, get ready to meet your new best friend: the picker.

In the old days, pickers generally worked on behalf of one or more local or national antiques dealers. But those days are changing. Now, for the most part, pickers work for themselves. By the way, pickers don't really want to be called pickers—they see themselves as dealers.

Believe me, these dealers aren't to be feared. You'll need them as much as you ever want to be wary of them. They are the oil in the machine, the wind in the sail, the cash on the barrelhead of the commerce you want to be a successful part of. And they are not out to get you. They are in the buy low and sell high game. Sure, some of them can be rude, obnoxious and pushy, but they also have a collective knowledge from which, if you are polite and ask some basic questions, you can gain benefit from. In the early days of my career as an estate liquidator, I relied on these folks to fill in the gaps of my lack of information, and many of them have become my friends.

• •

Taking the time to do research before your sale will help, but without outside expert assistance, you are doomed.

• •

Here are just a few kinds of things you may overlook as having value that pickers will love you for.

EPHEMERA: Ephemera basically means printed material not meant to be preserved or retained for any great period of time. But when you understand ephemera, or "old paper," which is what it's called in the antiques and collectibles business, the world of its beauty opens up, and there before you will be stacks of graphically cool magazines from the 1920s and '30s, sexy pin-up cal-

In the late 18th and 19th centuries, one of the most popular expressions of sentimentality was wearing jewelry containing human hair. Pieces like this pendant were worn as memento mori (mourning) and also as love tokens.

endars from the '50s and '60s, and every manner of soap and sewing trading cards ever created. That is just a small scrap of the old paper pile that can be found in a home that has definite value. For instance, the April 13, 1962 issue of *Life* magazine has a baseball card of Mickey Mantle and Roger Maris in it that is worth well over $100. There are *Spider-Man* #1 comics selling in less than mint condition for over $90,000. An original Honus Wagner baseball card in Very Good condition can be worth over $700,000 or more if it is in Mint condition.

But you are not going to know this when you start sorting through gramp's garage or Aunt Mary's attic. What you'll see is yellowing or soiled paper, the dog-eared pages of old brochures, old bits and pieces of advertising, and you'll think to yourself that it's a literal pile of junk. And what is worse than putting too much money in other people's pockets because of your lack of knowledge? Throwing items of value away, which is what a lot of you will be tempted to do, especially when it comes to those old paper piles. A lot of this never makes it to an estate sale because it is tossed away as junk.

But some of you will like the junk paper you find, put it all into a box or two, and save it for your sale, hoping others will also like the typeset, old-fashioned illustrations, and those gorgeous colors designers used to use. I guarantee that somebody in your town who loves ephemera will come to your sale, pick that box up and ask, "How much you want for this old paper?" And you may ask what they'll offer and they'll say $20 and you'll agree, satisfied that you got way more for that pile of musty paper than you thought you could. The picker, though, will have a grin to go along with their sense of satisfaction. They've bought well, and after selling your stuff to another dealer on eBay, their profits on a $20 purchase might earn them an income that others can't generate in a week, month, or year of labor.

COSTUME JEWELRY: Let's say that your grandmother, great aunt, or some other female relative in your family was really into costume jewelry. They liked the glitz of diamonds but couldn't afford them, so they bought rhinestone jewelry instead. Costume jewelry can't be worth much, right? Most of it is made from base metals and colored glass, not gold or silver.

So, you've gone through the jewelry box on top of the bureau, and some of you have also had the dread of going through whole chest of drawers filled with trays and boxes of costume jewelry, with the idea in mind that this stuff is not worth much.

You were careful, though, and made sure to remove any gold or silver jewelry you found, and you're thinking because the rest of the jewelry is costume, you don't have to really pay too much attention to its value. The jewelry ladies

Stay alert: This puffy heart silver charm bracelet is worth over $1,000; if each of its charms were enameled, it would sell for over $2,000.

who fanatically shop estate sales are smiling in cafes sipping expensive lattes, savoring the moment they'll get to paw their way through your mound of costume jewelry piled on some table in the middle of a sale. They can afford their leisurely repast. What do I mean by this? Even though the overwhelming majority of costume jewelry you find is worth only a dollar or two a piece, some of it is worth hundreds or in some cases thousands of dollars. These ladies know what you don't.

HERE ARE A FEW EXAMPLES:
- A Trifari sailboat brooch sold for $2,500 at Doyles on Nov. 16th, 2004
- A Coro seahorse duette sold for $2,000 at Doyles on April 11th, 2006
- A Bakelite-carved witch pin sold for $1,800 at Morphy's on Oct. 26th, 2010

LPS—PHONOGRAPH RECORDS: LPs, or records, are today thought of by most people as being too old a form of musical recordings to be of much use. Who even has a record player anymore? Most of us are not even using CDs anymore, instead preferring to listen to music on our smartphones, laptops, or computers.

When heirs come across a shelf of records in an estate, or even more horrifying to some, boxes and boxes of records stored in the garage or a closet, many will despair and wonder, "What in the world are we supposed to do with these?"

A number of years ago, I had the opportunity to sell a collection of 100,000 LPs. An older gentleman who lived far out in the country had collected them over many years. His isolated location was not a great place to stage a sale, so I rented a space at Fort Mason in San Francisco and transported all the records there. An experience I had there epitomizes for me what most people's attitudes about the value of phonograph records are. While I was outside the door of the space that we had rented, two young people came walking by, and looking at my sign advertising that I had records for sale, one said to the other, "Records? Who uses those things anymore?" They are not alone in that perception.

The fact of the matter, though, is there are still hundreds of thousands of people who regularly listen to and collect old phonograph records. Not only that, they also listen to and collect 78 rpm records. Don't know what a 78 is? A 78 record is a format for playing records that predates LPs. While it is true that most 78s, LPs, and 45s that you find in a home are not worth a lot of money, they will at least garner a dollar or two at your sale. The records that you have

Be on the lookout for blues, country and jazz 78s on Vogue, Black Patti, Black Swan, Autograph, Berliner, and Fonotipia record labels.

You will get picked if you don't fully embrace and understand the old maxim, 'One man's trash is another man's treasure.'

to pay careful attention to are the many out there that are worth hundreds, if not thousands, of dollars.

A stereo version of the record, "Introducing the Beatles," on the Vee-Jay label sold for $4,000 on Dec. 13th, 2011, at Heritage Auctions, Inc., and this is not the most valuable record out there. There are records worth over $10,000. I wouldn't concentrate on those numbers too much, though, as records worth that kind of cash are exceedingly rare. Concentrate instead on the fact that there are thousands of records out there, in everyday collections, worth between $5 and $100.

When we advertise that we have records or LPs in our estate sales, there will always be a number of dealers vying for a place at the head of the line. They're there because they just have to find out if we have a long lost prize, a record to fill the gap in one of their customer's collections. At your sale, they'll be looking for how you may have made a mistake.

I have only described three categories of items you might chance upon in a home, which could have immense value and be treasures in disguise, or that could very well enhance an estate's coffer. The real list of all the things you should be on the lookout for as an executor that you could sell for real money is long. Get help and don't do this all by yourself. It takes years to know about stuff or how to tell the difference between what has significant value and what is common and modestly valued.

THREE MAJOR REASONS YOU WILL GET 'PICKED'

1. YOU WILL GET PICKED IF YOU DON'T FULLY EMBRACE AND UNDERSTAND THE OLD MAXIM, 'ONE MAN'S TRASH IS ANOTHER MAN'S TREASURE.'

"It's all trash." "How could anyone collect so much garbage?" "Trash, there's a mountain of it!" I wish I could tell you how many times I have heard comments like these in the years I have been an estate liquidator. If there are treasures hidden, often you'll never know because as you progress through the whole clear-the-house-out project, you'll get tired and your fatigue may lead you to become judgmental or angry. These emotionally charged states are not conducive to generating positive results.

But who can blame you? You have a life. Your time spent toiling weekends or in the evenings after work on behalf of the estate you are responsible for is taking time away from what used to be the routine of your life. You might start to take it too personally. You might begin to lose your perspective and start to act too quickly, and thereby throw away valuable items to the ultimate pickers: the people who pick up your trash every week. They cart away more of value than any of your town's antiques and collectibles picker ever will.

We, as a matter of procedure, will go through the bags of trash our clients leave for us to dispose of. I am not talking about true trash here; the bags we are going through hold every kind of household item that you can imagine. People will throw these kinds of things away because they are steamrolling their way through to empty the house. They gather speed, forgetting how important it is that they take more time, and this haste leads to mistakes. It is not unusual for us to find many useable and saleable items in these bags, so we take them out of the bag, dust them off, add a price sticker, and sell them.

Never mind the *American Pickers* or the guys and gals who incessantly hunt for bargains at garage and yard sales—the first picker you want to avoid is the garbage man.

A TALE OF TWO HIGHBOYS:

- A Fine Queen Anne highboy was sold by Sotheby's on Jan. 20, 2007 for $228,000.
- A Good condition Queen Anne highboy was sold by Kaminski Auctions on Dec. 29th, 2010 for $36,000.

2. YOU WILL GET PICKED IF YOU THINK THAT YOU CAN RELY ON YOUR OWN RESEARCH ABOUT VALUES.

Presently in my research library, I have a vast collection of guidebooks, each detailing the specifications and suggested values for almost every conceivable antique and collectible that exists. Do you have these books? No? I didn't think so.

Professional pickers, antiques dealers, auctioneers, and estate liquidators pay subscription fees that enable them to access massive databases detailing the current market values of not just what is common, but also for what is rare. Do you currently have access to these databases? Do you want to pay to acquire access? I bet not.

Then there is the problem of analyzing the information that you find on the Internet or in books about antiques and collectibles. There are a hundred different shades of nuance between an item whose condition might be described as: Mint, Original or Fine, Very Good, Good, Fair, and Poor. Are you prepared to understand these differences? Good luck with that. It is not easy. Even I find

You will get picked if you skimp on or avoid paying professionals to inform you about an object's worth or to act as an agent for its sale.

these distinctions to be difficult to parse from time to time. These condition states may seem abstract to you and you could easily think there is not much of a value difference between Mint and Very Good, but you would be mistaken.

Please conduct your own research and most definitely try to understand both what an item is and what it may be worth. But don't ever believe that the results of your research reflect the entire body of information that there is to acquire about that item. That's what professionals, who have been at the business of appraising and conducting sales for years, get paid to analyze and inform you about.

3. YOU WILL GET PICKED IF YOU SKIMP ON OR AVOID PAYING PROFESSIONALS TO INFORM YOU ABOUT AN OBJECT'S WORTH OR TO ACT AS AN AGENT FOR ITS SALE.

Even if you decide that you're not going to have a professional stage your garage or estate sale, I strongly suggest that you hire one to help you better understand the value of your items. Call an estate liquidator, antiques dealer or a certified personal property appraiser and have them perform a walk through of your place. Listen to what they have to say. Take lots of notes and ask lots of questions.

These professionals have evidence-based appraising skills, as well as treasure hunting instincts that they have developed over many years of experience. They can see value where you may only see stuff. They are not tired, angry, or time pressured in the same way as you may be. Their minds are clearly focused on the single task of finding value, even if it has all along seemed hidden to you.

Your choices become clearer about how to market or sell an item once you first learn what an item really is. Knowledge is golden. If you have it already, great! If you don't, expect to pay for it.

If you decide that you want to save money by not paying the reasonable cost for an expert's sage advice, then expect to place the money you saved from not paying their fees, plus way more, into the pockets of pickers, who I guarantee will love you for it.

HOW TO NEGOTIATE WITH *PAWN STAR* WANT-TO-BES

The first thing to take firmly into consideration way before you think of approaching a pawnshop owner or an antiques dealer to sell your stuff is that they are not just experts in their specialized fields, but that they have also

A Xin Ling Blanc de Chine Fu dog.

become, out of necessity, practiced at the art of negotiating purchase prices that are as low as possible. This is their job and the way they make money. There is no way that they will pay you what an item is worth and then turn around and sell it for what it is worth. That's a zero-sum-gain transaction. They can't stay in business like that.

They have to be able to buy low, so that they can sell high. In order for them to make a profit, they need to negotiate as low of a purchase price with you as is possible. How low of a purchase price they pay you depends, in large part, on how informed you are. How informed you are about what the item is and what its value might be is only part of the process, though; you will also need to learn to haggle and negotiate. You need to keep in mind the Kenny Rogers song, "The Gambler": "Know when to hold them, know when to fold them, know when to walk away, know when to run." You are the one who ultimately decides to sell, keep, or go to another dealer and ask for other offers. For peace of mind, figure that you'll be going to at least two different dealers to listen to their offers.

The second thing you will want to take into consideration is that no matter how nice these professionals seem when you first meet them, or how honest and ethical their reputations purport them to be, the relationship between you and them is still of an adversarial nature. Even as you notice how cordial and polite they are, remember this is a business transaction; at the end of the day, you will hopefully part on friendly terms, but you will never be best buddies with them.

On some occasions, dealers will be so transparent about their business practices that they will inform you exactly what they think something is worth, and then give you an offer based upon that value. In any case, whatever they offer you will be somewhere between one and three quarters of what they think your particular item is worth.

Negotiating an acceptable purchase price for your item with an antiques dealer will proceed differently than with a pawn shop owner. For the most part, negotiating a high purchase price with a pawn dealer will be much more difficult. Much more!

Most of the time, your negotiations with pawn shop dealers will go something like this: You bring up to the counter a diamond ring you inherited from your grandmother, her words still ringing in your ears, "Take care of this ring. One day you may need to sell it. It's a big diamond, so don't sell it too cheaply." You also bring along the appraisal document your grandmother had made that lists the values of her jewelry. You are excited. Her appraisal document clearly states that the value of her ring is in excess of $12,000, so you naturally are surprised when the pawn shop offers you only $2,000.

When dealers, whether they are pawn shop or antiques dealers, have an item brought to them, they have to make four key buying decisions before they will agree to purchase your item.

1. Do I want or like this item?
2. Is there a market for this item?
3. What is this items condition?
4. How much will I have to pay?

You look into the eyes of the pawn shop operator and with your finger tapping the appraisal document, you say, "But this appraisal says the ring is worth $12,000." This is when you will learn one of life's painful lessons: an item's worth is not based upon the abstraction of value that an appraisal certificate states, but by the actual amount of cash someone is willing to pull out of their pocket to pay for it. This is otherwise known as "fair market value."

Let me just state for the record that it is unlikely that you will be able to sell your grandmother's ring to anyone but a consumer for anything like $12,000.

Let's contrast and overlay the four key buying decisions that a dealer has to consider in order to successfully purchase your grandmother's diamond ring for a price that will allow them to make a profit once they are able to re-sell it.

1. DO I WANT OR LIKE THIS ITEM? In the case of your grandmother's diamond ring, unless it is of a significantly large carat weight or has amazing color and clarity, I promise you that the dealer you are offering it to really doesn't care if they buy it. Most diamond rings that people bring into them on a daily basis are not valuable in the secondary diamond markets. So they may not be all that interested in buying your grandmother's ring unless they can purchase it for a low price. Most diamonds below one carat will be of little interest; the bigger the diamond, though, the more interest there will be in the secondary diamond markets.

2. IS THERE A MARKET FOR THIS ITEM? But let's just say that your grandmother's ring has a diamond in it that is well above one carat, and that its color, cut, and clarity are desirable—then you may have a good chance to sell this ring for a fairly high price, if this particular pawn shop dealer has a customer base willing to pay high prices for high-quality diamonds. If they do not have the right customer base, their offer will still be on the low side. There are high-end pawn shops out there. If you have a significant diamond ring, go to one of these shops first; at the very least, you will know that they have a customer base for high-end stones, and because of this, that they are in a position to offer much higher prices.

••

An item's worth is not based upon the abstraction of value that an appraisal certificate states, but by the actual amount of cash someone is willing to pull out of their pocket to pay for it.

••

3. WHAT IS THIS ITEM'S CONDITION? The ultimate place where negotiations may break down with pawn shop owners or antiques dealers will have to do with your item's condition. Let's say that the pawn shop owner you're trying to sell your item to likes and wants your grandmother's diamond ring, and has a market for it. The next thing they will need to determine is how fine the condition of the ring is. Condition affects value, so any scratch or chip to the diamond, however minor, the fact that any of the smaller stones are missing, or if the ring has ever been resized, will each become negotiating points for the pawn shop owner to use in order to negotiate a lower purchase price. When a dealer wants to buy an item, condition issues become their best reason to offer you less money. But on the other hand, when a dealer sells, oftentimes the so-called condition issues they disparaged so much about when purchasing the item in the first place becomes their proof that the item is old, has character, or was well loved. So it is important for you to remember that when it comes to issues of condition controlling a price negotiation, two people can play at that game.

A Teddy Roosevelt and the Bear mechanical bank sold at an estate sale for $550.

4. HOW MUCH WILL I HAVE TO PAY? Part of the calculus leading up to the decision of how much a pawn shop owner is willing to pay for your grandmother's diamond ring or for that matter any other item you may bring to them, is the ever changing dictates of the shop's regional marketplace. This is not just a clear mathematical formulation. I know you might want it to be, but some parts of a dealer's formulation about value are instinctual and emotional. In other words, their formulation for buying an item may not make complete sense to you, but it does to them. It is a combination of hard math mixed with sharp-eyed instincts.

THE CEILING AND FLOOR CONCEPT OF PRICE NEGOTIATION

In the simple purchase price negotiations you'll have with pawn shop owners or other dealers, there are only two negotiating concepts that you will need to keep in mind. These tactics or concepts are not only simple to understand, they are exceedingly simple to employ and they will most definitely assist you in reaching your goal of selling your grandmother's diamond ring for as much as is possible. By adopting this approach, you will have a fairly good chance of selling your item for as high a price as any dealer may be willing to pay.

If you are the first person to state a purchase price amount, then the ceiling and floor concept of price negotiation will look like this:

EXAMPLE A

THE CEILING: Any amount first stated by you becomes your ceiling price—the highest purchase price that your item has any chance of selling for. In order for you to proceed in this negotiation and get your item sold, you will need your counter offers to decrease in value.

DISADVANTAGE: If you are the first person to state a price, then you will never know what the other party's first offer may have been. It is possible that they may have been willing to make you a higher offer.

THE FLOOR: Any amount counter-offered by a dealer becomes their floor price—the lowest price your item might sell for. In order for the pawn shop owner to proceed in this negotiation and buy your item, they will likely need to increase in value their subsequent offers.

ADVANTAGE: Their first counter offer, or the floor, is a no-brainer for them. They can't lose by making their counter offer ridiculously low because your counter offer will invariably set up a new much lower ceiling price. So in just a few moments of negotiating, they have been able to get you to lower your expectations considerably.

If you can get the pawn shop owner or antiques dealer to be the first to state an offer, then the ceiling and floor concept of price negotiation flips, and will look like this:

EXAMPLE B

THE FLOOR: Any amount first offered by the dealer becomes the floor or the lowest price this particular item has a possibility of selling for. It is not the highest price they may be willing to pay. All of their subsequent counter offers will by necessity need to increase.

DISADVANTAGE: If the dealer makes the first offer, which by the way most of them are loathe to do, they are put in the unwelcomed position of having to increase their subsequent offers in order to purchase your item.

THE CEILING: Any counter offer stated by you even at this point in the negotiation still becomes the ceiling price.

ADVANTAGE: If you are able to get the dealer to make their offer at the onset of the negotiation, it is quite possible that this initial lapse of judgment on their part will reveal two important and critical things about their negotiating style. The first being, that if they're making their offer first, this could be a signal that they have a strong desire to purchase your item, they may be willing to pay more because of that desire. The second biggest advantage to having them make their offer first is that each of their subsequent counter offers to you have to be as increases of their first offer.

REMEMBER: YES AND NO ARE POWER WORDS

The two most powerful words in the English language that are central to moving any negotiation forward are the words "Yes" and "No." They facilitate or stall commerce like no other two words. Things happen, cash drawers slide open, checks are happily signed and trips get made to the bank after someone says the magic word "yes." On the other hand, when someone says "no," it's not as if something equally profound hasn't happened. To the contrary, something important has occurred: one side in the negotiation has taken a definite stance. Pay more, or I walk. You can say no. It's a simple word; use it.

ESTATE LIQUIDATORS, PICKERS, ANTIQUES DEALERS, AND PAWN SHOP OWNERS ARE NOT THE ENEMIES!

Ignorance is.

You must always remember that as an executor, it is your legal and moral duty to make sure that your decisions about the "stuff" in the estate you are working on provides the right answers to each of these four questions:

1. WHAT IS THE OBJECT: You really can't proceed with selling an item to anyone until you fully understand what the item is. If you can't figure it out, then you need to find someone who can. Selling an item without first identifying it is like gambling away part of your family's legacy. Ignorance has no place in the marketplace. Thankfully there are people more suited to the task of identifying an object's worth then you are. They can help you. I strongly urge that on behalf of your family, you make the necessary efforts needed to locate them.

2. WHAT IS THE BEST WAY TO SELL IT: When you finally know what an object is, and only then, you should begin to explore the various selling options that are available to you. In general, the higher the value of the item, the better the sales venue that should be sought out to sell that item. Your estate's highest-

You never know what you will find at estate sales, whether doll heads or a Steiff teddy bear.

value items should at the very least be consigned to the largest regional auction house in your area. If your estate is chock a block stuffed with high-value items, then seeking out the opinion of one of the large international auction houses is a definite must.

3. WHAT OUTSIDE HELP SHOULD I SEEK: Look up estate liquidators, appraisers, and auctioneers in your area. Interview them on the phone, and the ones that you feel most comfortable with, go ahead and set appointments with them so that they can make an on-site inspection of your premises. Seek out the opinions of more than one expert. Check their references. Read their contracts.

4. WHAT DATE WILL IT SELL BY: The time span between when you drop your items off at an auction house and when they finally offer your item up for sale can seem elongated. Auction houses have schedules, and lots of personal property to cycle through their calendar of sales. In general, the higher the value of the item or the more specialized of an object it is, the longer it will take to cycle through an auction house's schedule.

••

Estate liquidators, pickers, antiques dealers, and pawn shop owners are not the enemies. Ignorance is.

••

This is largely a function of the way auction houses create theme-based auctions. For instance, if you have a Navajo blanket, and it is special, that item will be placed in a Native American sale, and the auction house that you brought this item to may only have one or two Native American Themed sales a year. So it will take time for them to sell your item. Also, auction houses can take a long time to pay you. This is normal. All of them are on twenty- to thirty five-business-day payout schedules. If you need to sell your item in a hurry, then an auction may not be your best way to get income fast. Thirty five business days is a long time.

It is my sincerest wish that after you have read this chapter, you will have learned that it is you who is in charge of your decision making, that you do not have to take actions concerning an estate alone, and that there are many options available to you, which will aid and assist you to reaching your goals.

Chapter 4

·················

TRASH, JUNK OR TREASURE: WHAT'S THE DIFFERENCE?

MOST OF US THINK IT IS EASY to recognize what trash is. It's the stuff we put into plastic bags and then into receptacles which we roll out to the curb once a week for the trash guys to pick up, right? We've been throwing things away all our lives; of course we know what trash is. But what if there was stuff that we thought was trash, but it wasn't after all? And what if that stuff was worth bucks, but we didn't know until after the garbage truck had come and gone? Wouldn't that be like throwing money away? Would you be able to tell if the old postcard you are about to toss is worth $1,000 or fifty cents? I don't think so. So what is the difference between what is true trash and the junk you can sell?

THREE WAYS TO LOOK AT WHAT STUFF IS

Trash: Something without monetary or utility value you pay to dump.

Junk: Something you don't want and don't understand how anyone else might want, but does have utility to others, so much so that they are willing to pay money to buy it.

Treasure: Something previously unknown about and found amongst junk.

You would think the differences between these three distinctly different categories of items would be easy to sort out. But sadly, this is not the case. People get compressed for time. They get overwhelmed. And mad. They apply their own ideas about value to the items they are finding in the home, and then because they think those items are worthless, they throw them away. The question to ask is what about the way someone else might think about utility or value? Isn't this a better way to try and understand what should be termed trash and made distinct from what is saleable junk? What might someone else want? How much will they pay for your so-called junk?

In my career as an estate liquidator, I have been paid by clients to remove what they have called trash from their homes. These were places that had already been well searched through; supposedly there was nothing left in them of any value. I've been told take it all away, we never want to see that stuff again. And in some of those homes, I found much saleable junk; in some, I have found treasures.

This is an all-too common sight for millions of people.

In general, older quilts in good condition have greater value, and linens, embroidered or otherwise, are always popular sellers.

I am reminded of the guy who called a few years back and wanted me to sell all the furniture he had left in the house of his mother, saying, "I got rid of all the junk to make your job easier." When I asked him what he meant, he told me that he had bagged up all the small stuff in her house and was in the middle of taking loads of it to the dump. I asked him if he had any of it left and he said, "Yes, I have about 30 large garbage bags stacked in the garage ready to load for my next three trips." All I can say is that it was lucky for him that he hadn't hired a hauler and finished the job before I had the chance to look over his so-called junk.

I remember getting that sinking feeling, the one all estate liquidators get when they hear from clients like this, wondering, what has this man done and what items of value has he already thrown away? I asked him to stop with the dump runs and said I'd be right over.

•••

Just because you don't think an item has a desirable purpose doesn't mean it doesn't have one. One thousand items like this that you might want to throw away, when sold for a dollar each, equals $1,000. Do you want to throw a thousand dollars away?

•••

When I got there, I sat on a wooden chair in the center of his garage and started going through the trash. He thought I was a crazy man and wanted to know why was I going through the garbage. What there was of value was upstairs; it was the furniture he had saved, or so he thought. In the bags, I found sets of dishes, Baccarat crystal, vintage Fillmore West Handbills, and many knickknacks. This man had bagged up these items to take to the dump because his views about value were about how useful these items might be to himself, and because they had no usefulness to him, he had decided it all must be trash. Suffice it to say, I priced it, added it in with the furniture upstairs, and staged a nice little estate sale for him.

This has been my experience with greater frequency than you might think, to have found useful, valuable, or rare items buried beneath the avalanche of my clients' stuff. Success like mine at finding useful stuff that can be sold also happens to resourceful heirs and executors when they take the time to understand the difference between trash and junk.

Taking the time to separate saleable junk from what is trash or debris is part of the process of discovering treasure, and is a chore that has to be done. How do you know when something is trash or when it is junk? Let's remember that for our sorting process, we are defining the word "junk" as something you don't want but may have utility value to others. So, if you are the type of person who appends value to an item based solely on its utility to you, then you are going to need to revise that way of thinking in order to get through the process with your sanity, as well as to collect the income this effort is bound to generate.

Just because you don't think an item has a desirable purpose, doesn't mean it doesn't have one and that others won't find it useful. One thousand items like this that you might want to throw away, when sold for a dollar each, equals $1,000. Do you want to throw a thousand dollars away?

Let me further illustrate this: We all need decent pots and pans to cook our meals in, but do we all need an old cast iron ladle? No, but someone will buy it if they see it at an estate sale. We all need writing implements, pens, pencils, markers and so on, but do we all want a bag of used ones? No, but someone will buy it at an estate sale. And take care with that bag of pens you want to throw away, as some of them could be collectible. Most of us like to listen to music, but we have all our songs on MP3 players or our computers now, so do we need to listen to music on LPs or other sized vinyl records anymore? No, but someone will still buy these records at an estate sale.

The point that I am making is that there are thousands of different items that people will routinely find in their homes that they think have no value because these items have no value to them. They will throw this stuff away because they can't see how these items might fit into anybody else's life. This way of thinking is clearly mistaken! So, a redefinition of the concept of trash is in order. Trash is something no one, and I do mean no one, would possibly want for their own decorative, utilitarian, or resale purposes.

Think of yourself as someone not on a mission to take out the garbage, but a mission to discover hidden value. Your status as an executor requires this of you. You have been tasked with the responsibility by the decedent to maximize the value of their personal property—a thankless task at times to be sure, but one that leads to its own kinds of rewards.

TWO STORIES ABOUT TREASURES FOUND IN TRASH

EXHIBIT 1: OIL PAINTING FOUND AT THE DUMP

I have a friend, who wishes to remain anonymous, so I'll call him Tom. He is in his seventies now, and still an active buyer and seller at flea markets and monthly auctions. He is a true one-of-a-kind character, with his gray beard and eyes a twinkle. You might think he looks like an actor from an old Hollywood western, playing the part of the sun-beaten grizzled miner leading his burro up a twisting Sierra Madre trail. I love this guy, and in my early days as an estate liquidator, I had many fine conversations with him and learned much about the

Scenes painted at the top of antique trumeau mirrors are common, but check their signatures—occasionally you'll find one by a famous artist.

business as a result.

Tom has spent most of his years working at the low end of the antiques and collectibles marketplace, making a dollar or two from the dimes he spent; not a bad way to make a living. He's honest, makes his own hours, and doesn't have to answer to anybody. If you yourself are a bit shortsighted, or think you should only deal with people who carry around business cards, then you might dismiss Tom as just some old man. But Tom has stories about valuable things he's found in the trash—items that someone in your position once threw away.

One day while Tom was at a dump in the San Francisco Bay Area, unloading

When sorting through a loved one's possessions, expect to find surprises. These silver quarters are worth about twenty times face value.

what he would call "a bunch of crap," he noticed that just up the slope from him was a truck with a couple of day laborers tossing out what looked to be a whole load of household furnishings. People offloading entire households into dump pits is not all that unusual and happens just about every day, which is a tragedy, of course. Who knows what they're throwing away?

Tom began to intermittently watch them, checking to see if whatever they were tossing out might be candidates for him to retrieve and later resell. He watched as one of the guys threw an old-style suitcase into the air, which, upon landing, busted open, dashing into the debris a small, framed picture that had been stashed in it, and breaking the glass in the frame as well.

Without saying a word, Tom stopped what he was doing and picked up the picture and stowed it in the cab of his truck. Later, while in the comfort of his home, he examined the picture more carefully, noticing that in fact it was a painting. His wife took one look at the signature and confidently declared the small painting was by none other than Maynard Dixon. After some minor restoration and the replacement of the glass, Tom sold the painting to a dealer for more than $10,000, which made that trip to the dump a profitable one, indeed. Whoever threw that painting away obviously was in too much of a hurry.

EXHIBIT 2: CACHE OF COINS FOUND IN A RAT-INFESTED BARN

One day some time ago, I got a call from a fiduciary about a ramshackle house located in a toney neighborhood in Palo Alto, California, with a barn in the backyard. This house was one of the last old houses left in the neighborhood that had not been renovated or torn down in order to build a larger, more status-conscious home for some Silicon Valley tech type.

When I got there, I could see that this house, with its large barn, was totally out of character with the renovated architecture of the new homes in the neighborhood. The passage of hard times had left this house in poor condition and my client informed me that it and the barn were going to be torn down and the property sold.

The house was almost empty, save a few pieces of shabby furniture, and other than tossing those few pieces of furniture away, there wasn't much to do in the house. My client led me to the two-story barn. The first floor was filled with what mostly looked like debris, boxes, mechanical parts, and decrepit furnishings. The barn had an outside wooden stairway that we carefully climbed until we reached the door leading into what turned out to be a hodgepodge of second-floor rooms. It was a hot summer day. When my client unlocked and opened the door, the recognizable odor of rats mixed with the smell of sizzling hot tarpaper wafted forth from the door, all in an uninviting manner. Once we entered through the door, it took awhile for my eyes to adjust to the dimly lit surroundings enough to get a good look around. What I saw was even astounding to me, an estate liquidator, who thought he'd seen everything. Clearly I had not. Everywhere were boxes piled unstably high, broken furniture bits hung from the rafters, on the walls, framed photos strained to be seen beneath thick coats of dust. Spread all around, and more densely than you might imagine possible, were 40 to 50 years' worth of rat droppings. The now deceased owners many years ago had once owned a notions store somewhere in Palo Alto. When they closed that store down, they hauled its contents away, walking them up the barn's back stairs, and stored them into their already-crowded barn attic. Then they closed and locked the door and pretty much forgot all about it.

> **A gentle reminder:** Did you know that the aggregate value of the most common items found in a home often adds up to as much, and sometimes more, than the sale of the high-value items in an estate?

After a quick inspection in the boxes, we found some interesting old stuff, including vintage clothing, old sewing notions, tons of ephemera, bits and pieces of jewelry, and box after box of antique books. There was value here after all and items could be culled from the mess and sold.

When I first spoke with my client about her project, I had delicately suggested that it would be better for her and for her client if they hired me as a consultant—to have me come not as a buyer or hauler, but as someone who would act on behalf of her and the estate she represented to separate what was trash from what might have value. But she said no and just wanted the property cleaned out.

She wanted to hire my company to haul away what she called trash for a set fee. Essentially, she just wanted us to get rid of everything in the barn and make it disappear. In situations like that, I, acting in the capacity of a hauler, would then be free to keep anything my company found. But the first thing every client needs in situations such as this is to find an advocate, someone to be on their side and protect their interests. As I looked around, I started to feel even more like there were interests that needed protection.

Upstairs amidst the ruin of dust and debris, I renewed my insistence, trying to further persuade her to allow us to act on her behalf, holding up a few items and letting her know that they each had value—albeit modest, but values nonetheless. To her credit, she relented and agreed to hire us as consultants.

To make a long story short, after going through almost every last thing in the place and systematically sorting through and bagging up the trash, I arrived at the final corner of the final room upstairs in the barn and saw a small galvanized trash can with a lid. It was about 20 inches tall and had a wire handle with a black wooden handgrip. The first thing I noticed was how heavy the can was, and after all the work that we had done in this particularly filthy environment, it was the furthest thing from my mind that there could be anything of value in that can. But of course I had to check.

I wish that I could tell you how excited I was to find out what might be in the can, but you have to remember this was a dirty place and I was covered head to toe in soot. I pretty much just wanted to go home, but with a gloved hand, I lifted the lid. Because of the can's weight, I had thought that it might contain lead fishing weights or sand, so I was surprised to see it was instead filled to the brim with many small plastic bags, each one full of dimes, quarters, half dollars, and dollars; and all of them were minted pre-1964 and made of silver. Not bad for a full day of work trying to bring light into the gloom of swirling dust particles shrouding that upstairs room.

Suffice it to say, my client was a happy fiduciary after that. The 2012 value of those coins was between $40,000 to $50,000.

Take heed and caution. Mistakenly identifying your stuff as just trash will cost your estate plenty. But you may think these two stories are "one-off" experiences, exceedingly rare, and won't happen to you. Below, please find three more examples where it did happen to others:

THREE EXPENSIVE PAINTINGS DISCOVERED IN THE TRASH

- *Tres Personajes* by Rufino Tamayo: Sold for $1,049,000 at Christie's
- Painting by Edgar Payne: Sold for $187,000 at John Moran
- *Children Under a Palm Tree* by Winslow Homer: Offered by Sotheby's for £150,000 ($227,820 US)

ITEMS YOU MIGHT FIND AND THINK HAVE NO VALUE

SOLD FOR:
$6,000

GEORGE OHR POTTERY
Crumpled Bowl
Sold by Craftsman Auctions for $6,000

I absolutely love this example. Before I got into this business and had the good fortune to learn as much as I have, I had never heard of George Ohr and wouldn't have dared believe this bowl was worth any amount more than a few bucks. I am even sure I would have thought that this crumpled pot was on the wrong side of ugly. It wouldn't have been something I would ever have rushed out and hired an appraiser to evaluate.

TIP: Just because you think an item doesn't have value, it doesn't mean that others won't pay big dollars for it.

SOLD FOR:
$9,500

GRUEBY TILE

Incised Polar Bear Tile
Sold By Craftsman Auctions for $9,500

At 5-1/2 inches by 7 inches, this little Grueby tile, incised and modeled with a polar bear on an iceberg, is worth a whopping $246 a square inch. OK, so it's nice enough, but really no big deal right? Maybe you would think it wasn't exactly trash and give it to a friend who stopped by and happened to admire it. Or perhaps you might drop it off at the Goodwill.

TIP: Just because it looks simple doesn't mean that only a simpleton would buy it. It is actually difficult to create simple. In the case of The Grueby Tile Co., its output became the standard against which all early 20th century Arts and Crafts potters compared themselves.

SOLD FOR:
$10,000

DIRK VAN ERP COPPER VASE

Sold by Clars Auction Gallery for $10,000

"Old copper vase with dents." That is how you might describe this 12-inch tall vase. It is damaged, it has a dent, and not a small dent, either. Junk, right? Worth a couple of bucks, maybe $30 or $40 tops, right? To understand the value of any one thing, you have to take yourself out of the equation. Its value is not about how much you might pay; it's about how much others might pay. An item's worth or its significance to collectors is based on their ideas about value, not your own.

Once upon a time while doing a walk-through of a home located on the wealthy island of Belvedere in the San Francisco Bay, I discovered a large Dirk Van Erp bowl being used as a water catch under a downspout. It had been outside suffering the elements for years. It was a true wreck and streaked green by water and age. This bowl had lost its curbside appeal. Collectors wouldn't want it, right? But even in terrible condition, and I do mean terrible, I sold that bowl for $475. Not a fortune, but still income.

TIP: Always, always, always look for identifying marks on items, and then look those marks up before deciding if your item has value. In the case of the Dirk Van Erp vase above, you will be looking to see if your hand-hammered copper items have an impressed Windmill mark.

SOLD FOR:
$2,200

TORN AND BATTERED BATMAN #1

Sold By Tory Hill Auctions for $2,200

This comic book was a definite candidate for the debris pile. It had no cover, was missing its centerfold, and many of its pages were dog-eared, soiled, and torn. Some little kid loved this comic to shreds, but for some reason, it survived. I am guessing there were countless attempts by his orderly mom to throw it away when he wasn't looking, and put it, along with his slingshot, into a trash can.

TIP: Stay open to discovery and be a detective. Some tattered and torn items have value.

TREASURES ARE WHERE YOU FIND THEM: SOMETIMES RIGHT UNDER YOUR NOSE

To know what a treasure is, you will have to understand a set of highly nuanced and arcane attributes, which will seem arbitrary at best. A found stash of cash, a retrieved diamond ring, a jar of gold coins—that these are treasures is obvious. What might not be obvious as treasures are the paintings found in dusty attics or the rare book that somehow got sandwiched between a series of dime store novels on the hallway bookshelf.

Because of a story that's been handed down like a myth in the family, you may know or have heard that somewhere in the house is a treasure. Dad hid money. Mom didn't trust banks. Uncle was an adventurer. And if you find what they've hidden, and you should definitely look, you will have located a treasure to be sure. Treasures, though, true spectacular edge-of-your-seat mysterious treasures, those might not look like treasures to you at all. I'll call these surprise treasures. That is why I caution you to go slow when liquidating an estate. Take your time. Get outside help. Hire experts.

Surprise treasures will look unassuming, common, or even ugly. Each one will look different and unique. They might be found in plain sight or extracted from deep between the layers of what anybody else in their right mind would consider as pure junk—I know that's where I've found a number of them. By their very nature, treasures are items that have eluded discovery, that have been hidden away, that have been forgotten. That's why you have to look for them because they are not obvious, at least at first.

BUT WHAT DO YOU CARE ABOUT TREASURE?

You are facing a mountain of stuff. A house so packed with someone else's belongings that there is scarcely room to squeeze another hankie out of the linen closet.

You're looking at kitchen cabinets packed way too tight with mugs bought on vacation and incomplete sets of chipped dishes. Scratched and chipped porcelain serving pieces seem to be more plentiful than bowls that are in good or useable condition. From the lower cabinets come tall stacks of sticky Tupperware, handleless burnt-out Teflon pans and cheap colored glass vases.

Make sure you double check all items before filling up any trash bags because it's so easy to overlook an item that may be valuable.

In the beginning, you entered the house with the best of intentions. You could do this. It wasn't going to be so hard. Maybe it would even be fun. So you took a few days off from work thinking it won't take too long, but then it does take too long. Your efforts are not making much of a dent, and you are becoming more frustrated by the minute. Maybe you start to get angry because you are starting to lose it. More and more, the contents of the home start to look like nothing but pure unmitigated trash.

Think of yourself as someone not on a mission to take out the garbage, but a mission to discover hidden value.

The word trash starts to issue forth from your lips more than a few times a day, your energy has begun to wane, you've started to feel defeated, and drained. The dump is starting to seem like such a great and wise alternative. You're certainly not alone in coming to this conclusion. Last year, hundreds of thousands of people in your situation called a hauler in and had them cart the whole sorry mess away. Who would blame you for giving in to the convenience of the dump?

No sane person wants to do what you have to. The dump solution is so simple, so immediate, and with just one little phone call, you can eliminate the dreary of so many endless days of soul draining and emotionally taxing work. Then you can put the cleared-out house on the market and get back to your life. Sounds good, doesn't it? Who would say no to such an easy solution? You should! Don't believe me? Call five estate liquidators in your area and ask them how advisable it is for you to begin the process yourself, of throwing things away. Their answers, I assure you, will be illuminating.

Chapter 5

CAN YOU REALLY SELL A ROLLS ROYCE OR A BOX OF CEREAL AT AN ESTATE SALE?

YES, YOU CAN SELL a Rolls-Royce, or a Maserati for that matter, at an estate sale. And yes, you can sell a cereal box, too, especially if it's a collectible Wheaties cereal box. In fact, most items found in a home sell well at an estate sale.

If you are not a professional estate liquidator, or have never been to or conducted your own yard sale or garage sale, then you may not be the best person to determine what can and cannot be sold at an estate sale. It'll seem crazy to you what people will buy, and how much they will pay for even the most common everyday objects. While talking to your spouse or some other family member after the sale, you'll say, "I still can't believe that they bought that."

If you are harried or time constrained, you may begin to make decisions that are less than optimal about what items in a house are sellable. If you think something is unusable, then you'll probably figure that the item is not usable by others. These are positions arrived at by people who don't fully understand the estate sales marketplace.

Throwing away usable stuff that can be sold is also a position that gets arrived at by stressed out people who feel they have way too much to accomplish in too short of a time frame, so they start throwing things away, almost as if the act itself could silence inner screams of rage or despair. Yes, I just wrote that. People, because they are angry, will go through a house rapidly and wildly toss stuff out as a reaction to feelings they just don't want to deal with. I call any of the above "tossing or cussing out dollars."

Ask yourself how much money you are willing to throw away and what of value you would rather donate then sell? This chapter is not about trash per se, nor is it about treasure. It's about how, if you include common everyday items into your sale, the kinds of things you may be tempted to throw away or donate, you will be positively adding additional streams of income into your estate, and contributing to its overall financial well being.

But they're old dolls you say; kitchen pots and pans, everyday dishes, cleaning supplies, mops and brooms, boxes of old linens, all the clothing in the closets, yard furniture and tools in the garage, and you're thinking that you can't sell that junk because you certainly wouldn't buy it. Yes, it's true, you might not buy it, but others will. Let's not mix up your lack of a need for an item with the very real probability that there are others, who not only have a need for the item, but have actually been looking for it and are willing to pay cash to purchase it.

Knowing the difference between "Southwest style" and what is truly Native American will enhance your estate sale's income.

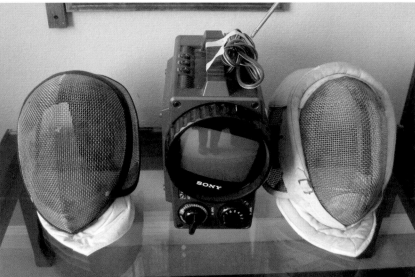

It's the "mix" of old and new, moderately valued with what is very valuable that leads to a successful estate sale.

In hand, you have your mother's diamonds and the rest of her jewelry. You have a good idea about the values of the artwork hanging on the walls of the hallway. The sterling and fine china have been located in the dining room. You're thinking of keeping your grandfather's gold watch; you also have an insurance appraisal document detailing the values for other items found in the home. So you're thinking, "I'm good, I'll just put my attention on what I already know to be valuable."

It's important that you give attention to items that you know to be valuable, but please consider the revenues that we generate from our estate sales can almost be evenly divided into two categories: income derived from the sale of high-valued items, and income derived from the sale of modestly valued items—the sort of items that sell for less than $20.

••

If you have never conducted your own yard sale, then you may not be the best person to determine what can be sold at an estate sale. It'll seem crazy to you what people will buy and how much they will pay for even the most common objects.

••

At our company, we call these two categories of stuff wheat and chaff. Wheat is the stuff you already think has value, so you are protecting it by not throwing it away, and chaff is the stuff you think has little or no value that you are contemplating donating or throwing away. But hold on a minute and try not to be in too much of a hurry. You just read that as much as half of the income from the estate sales that we conduct comes from the sale of the inexpensive, modestly valued personal property we find in homes—the kinds of things that a lot of people in their haste to get through the process as quickly as possible are thinking of giving or throwing away. All that little stuff when sold adds up to real money when it has been included into an estate sale. If the sale of your silver, china, and collectibles adds up to $5,000, that means the sale of all the small little stuff in your house has a great chance of being worth $5,000, too. Still want to throw away or donate a bunch of stuff?

Between the lines of this chapter's title are the thousands of things found in homes that have low to medium values. To understand that they have value, particularly if you are the type of person who has a minimalist approach to furnishing a home, or if you're the type of person who would never consider buying anything used, then you'll need to use a little imagination. If it helps, try this: Add a $ symbol in front of all the items you are thinking have little or no value. Now multiply that $ symbol by the number of items you're thinking of donating or throwing away. Now how much of this do you want to throw away or donate?

Unless your estate needs the cash, the income lost from donating or tossing away 500 one-dollar items is not a big deal. But what if you threw or gave away 500, five-dollar items? That's $2,500. Maybe you don't need $2,500, but do you really want to give or throw it away?

Give care to the details and remember that by including low and modestly valued items in your sale, you are adding to the overall income that can be derived from an estate sale. Also, there is a link between the sale of high-value items at an estate sale and the sale of these low and modestly valued items.

SOLD FOR:
$150

These fake marked Royal Vienna urns, though damaged, still sold at an estate sale for $150.

Victorian-era cranberry glass lusters, offered along with everyday common items, makes for an exciting sale.

We call this "letting the best sell the rest, and the rest selling the best." These two groups of items go hand in hand and enhance the sale of each other. There will be time later after the sale to make decisions about donating or throwing things away.

A BIC PEN BOX OR A STASH FOR CASH?

Ever since the first day I started my career as an estate liquidator, I have known that my primary objective on behalf of my clients was to generate for them the maximum amount of income possible from the sale of the personal property contained within the estates they represented. I knew this long before I knew a thimbleful of what any of my competitors knew, before I ever acquired much knowledge about antiques and collectibles. I knew that stuff, even if it was only minor stuff, had potential buyers for it, that income for the estate could be

Victorian mantle clock with faux
ormolu sold at an estate sale.

generated from the sale of just about anything.

Because this was my ethic, it meant to me that I could not leave a stone unturned pursuing asset maximization as my agenda, that I had to leaf through every last book on the bookshelf for hidden stashes, which is how I learned about book safes, but that's another story. It was important to me then, as it is now, that everything in a house gets labeled and priced, which naturally meant that I had to handle everything. In order to handle and price everything in the house, I had to slow way down, which led to greater calm and a better ability to pay attention to what I was doing. This had the ancillary benefit of leading me to some interesting and valuable discoveries. It's when you slow down that you find valuable stuff you didn't know you were looking for.

I was in a house where everything of value had already been discovered by the family, or so they thought. They had churned through the entire house and apparently found whatever it was they were looking for, and satisfied with their efforts, called me. People do this to estate liquidators every day—leave

HERE IS WHAT I CALL MY "SORTING ORDER OF LIQUIDATION."

1. **Try to sell it:** To generate the highest possible incomes for your estate, and save money from pre-sale debris removal cost, first try and sell stuff.

2. **Can't sell it? Donate:** Just because somebody didn't buy it at your sale doesn't mean that what remains is trash. Now that the sale is over, you or your estate liquidator can make arrangements to have your estate's remainders removed to a charity, as a donation.

3. **Can't sell or donate? Trash it:** There is definitely going to be debris left over after the estate sale and donation process. It is just a fact of life. Every home contains items that can be sold, ones that can't be sold, but can be donated, and items that cannot be sold or donated. This last group, as your or your liquidator's final act, will need to be removed to a landfill.

them with what might be referred to as the dregs, the unwanted stuff they are not interested in enough to keep. And we, being the magicians that we are, because we know how to identify such a wide variety of items, make mountains out of molehills.

Nothing in the house, right? Value all found, right? Just stuff left, right? Not quite. Upstairs in the top drawer of the master bedroom dresser amongst hankies, key chains, pads of paper, and so on, was a Bic Pen box. In that box were 100 $100 bills. Ten grand in all. Who knew that a small cardboard box meant to hold pens could contain so much cash? I do now ...

The reason this story is so important is not because it's an illustration about luck or fortune or to show how great I am. It's to show how there is a success link between certain actions. When you decide to give value to small things, and slow down enough to do so, big things have a better chance to follow.

At first glance, the contents of the drawer looked to consist of small inconsequential items that get used every day, but aren't thought of as having any financial value. No one would pay much more than a dollar or two for any single item that was in that drawer. It was just stuff. Someone less discerning, who hadn't the experience, especially if this drawer of stuff was the hundredth one that they had had to go through, might have just tipped the drawer up and over and emptied its contents into a large opened and inviting garbage bag; this happens every day.

So again, slow down and take a little extra time. Paying close attention pays dividends. The effort it takes to handle and carefully sort through the marginally valued items adds to an estate sale's overall bottom line, as well as sometimes generating the experience of discovering a Bic Pen box stuffed with cash.

THE IMPORTANCE OF BEING EARNEST

How come I'm going into such detail about what can and cannot be sold at an estate sale?

On January 5, 2013, I was in the home of an elderly lady's brother. It was a small house, by modern standards, in the Golden Gate Heights Area of San Francisco. It overlooked the entire expanse of "The Avenues." You could see the streets laid out block by grid pattern block all the way to the beach. It gets cold and windy up there, and even though there is plenty of residential density, it's surprising how few San Franciscans ever find their way along the curving bank of its hillside. It's quite spectacular.

I met my client standing in the open doorway of her brother's garage. I could see into the gloom of the garage, with its piles of paper, old boxes, filing cabinets, and all the hodgepodge of the 65 years her brother and his wife lived there.

When I get a phone call from someone, I ask them a lot of questions about the house's contents, so I can figure out whether there really is enough financial value in a house for me to take the time to visit it. I know that can be thought of as cold and calculating, and maybe it is, but given what I know and the experiences I have had dealing with marginally valued estates in the past, I have learned that I can only really help people whose estates have a large enough value profile to pay for our services. Unless there is a certain dollar component inherent in the estate, I will be unable to help. I just don't have the time. No one in the estate liquidation business does.

....

Unless your estate needs the cash, the income lost from donating or tossing away 500 one-dollar items is not a big deal. But what if you threw or gave away 500, five-dollar items? That's $2,500. Maybe you don't need $2,500, but do you really want to give or throw it away?

....

On the phone with her, she described her experience as being "a terrible time" clearing out the house. She told me that she and her nephew had already spent six months going through the house. This is not music to an estate liquidator's ears. We know that if you've spent that much time going through the house, you may have removed or retained so much that there may not be enough left in the house for us to do an estate sale. Retaining items for personal use or because specific items have been bequeathed to various family members is fine; it's what gets thrown away that poses the greatest financial threat to an estate.

But there was something sweet, innocent, and fragile about her. That's the crux of it, the very point I am trying to make here is about the fragility. That's the reason I'm putting such effort into asking you to take your time and think about the kinds of issues that this chapter is outlining. Too often people in the position of having to empty out a lifetime's worth of accumulations from a family member's home are, or can be, at some time during the process as fragile as this little old lady. When you're fragile, stressed, or emotionally drained, you are liable to make poor decisions or even tremendous mistakes.

After meeting and chatting with my client, I looked around the garage, as well as its connecting basement rooms, then went up the wooden stairs to the main floor of the house. The upstairs was small, with its two bedrooms, combination living room and dining room and small kitchen. What was interesting was what was not in the house. Where were the books missing from the shelves in the second bedroom which had been converted for use as an office? After all, an academic had lived in this house. Where were the stacks of folded and

Vintage clothing in good condition, as well as certain furs, do very well when sold at an estate sale.

What of value might be found in a closet? How about a pair of vintage Gucci driver moccasins worth about $200 at an estate sale.

embroidered linens? What happened to most of the dishes or the sterling that had once graced their dining table? They were gone and there was not much of value left. Where it might have all gone, I do not know. But there were some interesting things still left in the house: Persian carpets, Chinese porcelains, and other decorative items as well. So, on that basis, plus the fact that she agreed to allow us to supplement her sale with items from other estates, I agreed to help her. If there had been even $1,000 less in value in the estate, I wouldn't have been able to help her—that's how close to the margins her project was.

Sitting with her at her brother's dining table as she filled out our contract, I could see her become more relaxed; a load or weight was being lifted from her. She was going to get through this after all. Someone had come to help. She told me, "I don't really want to tell you this, but earlier in December after coming home from working in my brother's house, I was in such a fit of despair that I wanted to kill myself. I am so happy and relieved that you will take this project on, and now I can go home with the freedom of knowing that this problem has been taken care of."

This is a story that could have had a different, less happy ending. Her particular project, because so much had either been retained or thrown away, was only marginally valuable; almost not enough to attract the services of a professional or to encourage them to take on her burden as their own.

LET THE BEST SELL THE REST, AND THE REST SELL THE BEST

There is a definite success link between the sale of your estate's higher-value items and the sale of your estate's common or modestly valued items.

It never ceases to amaze me when one of our longtime customers, who has always been conservative and modest about what they purchase, suddenly becomes determined to buy something valuable. Conversely, it is not uncommon for customers, who come to our estate sales to spend as much money as they can, change direction and buy an item of modest value.

Sometimes high-profile buyers who come to our estate sales to purchase our advertised gold or silver or high-priced china sets will check those items out, but after viewing them, determine for whatever reason that they'll pass on buying. These buyers will then shop the rest of our estate sale looking for little things that they might need for their own homes or businesses and if they find one, will buy it. If we did not have the higher-valued items in the home in the first place, we never would've attracted these buyers. They figure, "I am here now, I might as well see what's in the rest of the house."

The other side is equally true: Shoppers who normally are in the marketplace for common everyday items sometimes become intrigued with a particular high-value item that we are selling. When shoppers who usually only buy low-value items see a high-value one they just have to have, they will often figure out how to buy it.

This is also true in the auction world.

In order to get a regional auction house interested enough in helping you with an estate's low or modestly valued items, it is helpful to remind them that when they are agreeable to the handling of your estate's lower-value items that they are making it easier for you to make the decision to allow them to be the auctioneer for your estate's higher-value items. You can use this strategy as leverage with either auctioneers or estate liquidators to good effect.

There is a link and I'll say it again: Let the best sell the rest, and the rest sell the best.

EVERYDAY HOUSEHOLD ITEMS THAT GENERATE ESTATE SALES INCOME

While it's obvious, at least to most people most of the time, that the value of the estate they're working with will be enhanced through the sale of its higher-valued items, consider the additional income that can be generated by adding to your sale the items below, plus more not listed, rather than donating or throwing them away.

KITCHEN: Pots, pans and grills, plates, dishes of all types—mugs, and cups, knives, spoons and forks, cooking utensils, measuring cups and spoons, chef and other knives, platters, bowls and other serving vessels, thermoses, kitchen counter appliances such as blenders, mixers, slot toasters, microwave and toaster ovens, food storage containers including canisters made from metal, glass, porcelain or wood, major appliances like stoves and refrigerators.

GARAGE: Hand and power tools, even if they are somewhat greasy, wooden and metal boxes—any toolboxes, nuts, bolts, screws and nails, as long as they are in some sort of container—auto parts, especially if they are vintage, and you know the make, model, and the year of the car they were made for, mason jars, other vintage canning jars, old magazines, wood piles, old brass and copper findings and hardware, lampshades, rope and other tie downs.

DINING ROOM: Napkins, tablecloths, glassware, bottles, vases, tinware, trays, salt and pepper shakers, pepper grinders, playing cards, glass pitchers, glass stoppers, coasters, placemats.

LIVING ROOM: Books, media of all types including LPs, CDs, VHS tapes, DVDs, bells, cheap figurines, lighters, ashtrays, sheet music.

BEDROOMS: Bedding, linens, sheets, clothing of all types, shoes, handbags, perfume containers, old and interesting printed hangers, vintage eyeglasses, vintage shaving items, costume jewelry, interesting vintage trash cans, compacts, hat pins.

CLOSETS: Office supplies, sewing supplies, scissors, holiday decorations, old cameras, bolts of fabric, rolls of vintage wallpaper, frames, suitcases, old yardsticks, games of every type, pillows, plastic boxes, plastic flowers.

GARDEN: Garden pots made from clay, porcelain, glass, metal, plant stands, plant hangers, small outdoor storage sheds, concrete birdbaths, animal figures, sundials, garden benches, shears, spades, rakes, hoes, other gardening equipment, outdoor furniture, tables, chairs, barbecue grills, and portable fire pits.

WHAT I WON'T SELL AT AN ESTATE SALE

GUNS AND AMMO: Laws vary state-by-state concerning the legality of selling guns and ammunition by non-licensed persons. In California where we conduct estate sales, it is definitely not legal, so the public sale of firearms or ammunition on behalf of our clients is not a service that we can offer them.

Once upon a time, though, early in my career, we had a client who had a collection of firearms he wanted us to sell, so we gave it a try. We advertised as part of our estate sale's announcement that on the evening of the first day of our sale we would offer this collection of firearms—on the condition that the transfer of ownership would have to be handled via a licensed firearms dealer.

Just to keep things safe, we took the extra precaution of hiring an armed off-duty police officer and a master of, I kid you not, Kung fu. It all worked out, which goes to show that it can. However, and this could be different depending on the area where you live, we found that the public sale of firearms during an estate sale brought levels of complication and expense to our company that we weren't willing to deal with again. So since that time, all the firearms or ammunition that we have found in the homes we're working in are removed for outside sale via a licensed firearms dealers or specialty auction house.

PORNOGRAPHY: Within at least 80 percent of all the homes I have ever worked in, there has been some level of material that could be described as either erotic or pornographic. Erotica I have no problem selling, as long as we prevent it from being viewed or sold to minors.

Most erotic material is fairly modest when compared to hard-core pornography. Pinup art from the 1930s through the 1960s, antique nude photographs, sex manuals or how-to guides from the late 1800s to early 1900s are all fairly innocent and can easily, at least in my opinion, be sold without moral objection. Any person who finds themselves in this position, whether they are a professional estate liquidator or an everyday person conducting their own family estate sale, needs to check with their own moral compass about the sales of erotica and let that be their guide.

The sale of hard-core pornography, though, is different and there may even be local blue laws in your area that either limit or outright ban your ability to sell this material. We're not talking about old *Playboys* from the 1950s here, which by the way can have significant value; we're talking about what most people would describe as smut.

One other type of erotic or pornographic material to be mindful of is mate-

Authenticating a Bottega Veneta handbag is not so hard. A purse by Chanel, on the other hand, is more difficult. This one was real and sold for over $500 at an estate sale.

SOLD FOR: $500+

These are specialty planes used in the making of violins. The group of these has a value of $450.

rial or photos of the decedent that are of a private nature. As an executor, you definitely want to be on the lookout for media containing these compromising images and have them removed from the house, preferably before allowing anyone else in, and this includes disallowing their being viewed by other family members as well.

PERSONAL ITEMS: Non-antique personal photographs, personal items of hygiene, sex aids of any kind, bedpans and portable potties, non-vintage or non-packaged lingerie, panties, bras, men's underwear, personal diaries, personal papers, bank statements, financial documents, personal letters or correspondence, prescription drugs, any item that would or could be construed in any way to cause shame or embarrassment to the decedent or their families.

HATE MATERIAL: It is unwise to offer for public sale material that promotes terrorism, hate, or violence. While it is true that there are types of so-called hate material that have historical value to archives, libraries, or other institutions, great thought and special care needs to be given to the disposition of material such as this. Putting hate material out at an estate sale, even when it has value, can cause controversy or outright hostility and may have a negative impact on your sale. Also, materials such as this can reflect poorly on the decedent or their family, and for that reason alone, its sale should be pursued through other channels.

FOOD: For us, there is too much liability that can arise from selling foodstuffs at our estate sales, so we don't, and we advise you not to either. I know there are some in the estate liquidation business who think it's perfectly fine to sell canned goods or other pre-packaged and sealed food items, but for us, it's not something we do. Some of this food will still have a theoretical shelf life left, though, and if that's the case, in order to have a good conscious about it, we suggest that you donate these foodstuffs to a local food bank.

BROKEN ITEMS: The only reason we ever knowingly sell an item that is broken or in need of repair is when that item's intrinsic antique or collectible value still has the potential to be realized as income. Old TVs? Donate them to Goodwill. Especially be wary of anything electric or with a frayed cord: light fixtures, stereo equipment, and any appliances with faulty wiring should be removed from the sale. If your damaged electrical item has value because it is an antique or collectible, it is best to find a way to remove its cord. This is the only way you can be certain that one of your shoppers won't plug it in to test it out while in your home or in theirs. In general, if you are going to sell items with any known condition issue, it is a good idea to let your buyers know about them.

DANGEROUS CHEMICALS: Garages, basements, attics and sheds are notorious areas within which homeowners think nothing of storing their chemicals; out of sight out of mind. Chemicals such as paints, solvents, gardening poisons,

Great care needs to be used when handling chemicals and other toxic materials.

industrial supplies and so on, do in fact pose health risks, not only for the family of the estate, but also for the estate sale's buying public. Great care and caution needs to be exercised when handling materials of a chemical nature. Also, for the most part, items that are chemical in nature don't really sell well, and when you add to that the fact that these chemicals may have safety, as well as environmental impacts, it is our strong recommendation that you do not offer them for sale.

ALCOHOL: Many states prohibit the sale of spirits including the sale of fine wine by any person who is not licensed to do so. Therefore, it is our recommendation that you engage, especially in situations where estates contain high-value spirits, or rare vintages of wine, the services of a competent alcohol consignment or brokerage service. Experts in the appraisal and selling of fine wine and spirits also have a far better chance of gaining for the estate higher prices for items like this than you can.

IVORY: Laws are changing all the time in relationship to the sale and distribution of ivory, even if it's provable that your ivory is truly of vintage and more hopefully of antique age. The burden of proof is very high and it is not cheap to obtain the proper appraisal documentation which will allow you to sell your antique ivory legally.

The fines that you might have to pay should you be caught selling ivory in a state where it is prohibited or where its sale is highly restricted is much higher, more often than not, than the value of the ivory itself. Ignorance of the law will not stop you from either being fined or having the ivory that you're trying to sell confiscated. In California, as well as in other major markets around the country, ivory is being confiscated from antiques stores, flea markets, and auction houses.

It is our strong suggestion that you contact your local auction houses or one of the specialty auction houses, if need be, to consult with one of their specialists, making sure to ask them if their firm can facilitate the legal sale of your vintage or antique ivory.

ITEMS WITH MOLD: I know you keep a clean house and so did your mom and dad, but here is an insider's point of view: somewhere in every house there is mold. Sometimes it's just a little bit, and sometimes it is so way over the top that the walls are streaked with it. In rooms or basements where there is the presence of mold, it is a strong possibility that the items found in those spaces, like books, paper goods, and upholstered items will also contain mold. I know you want to sell the stuff, but you have to take into consideration that items with mold in them sold by you to someone who's unsuspecting causes the mold contained in that item to contaminate the homes of your buyers. Mold migrates and spreads. Books containing mold in them will spread mold to other books and the same goes with furniture; a couch with mold will spread its mold into other pieces of furniture, drapes, and carpets.

DISTURBING GRAPHIC MATERIAL: There are so many categories of items that may be found in a home that could be considered by some as having a disturbingly graphic nature that it would be hard to list them all. Most of these kinds of items are harmless and are not by themselves promoting aberrant behaviors or misguided social agendas. I'm thinking of death photos, disaster photos, war photos, propaganda material from almost any time period, lynching photos, car crash photos, medical photos – those of operations, disfigurements or skin diseases, and many more.

It's not that they're not interesting because they are. Each of these has their own collector bases and many have significant values depending on their historical value, which probably makes a better case that they should go to a specialty auction house, rather than having them be included in your estate sale.

TAXIDERMY AND FURS FROM ENDANGERED SPECIES: Any article of clothing containing the fur from an exotic or endangered species should be eliminated from your estate sale. I have looked in closets and found jackets, stoles, and coats made from any number of what today are considered endangered species. When these items were first made in the 1920s, '30s, and '40s, they were considered exotic and highly desirable. Today, even though to some they may still be desirable, trading in pelts and furs of animals on the endangered species list is not only "politically incorrect," it is a sales activity that may bring with it the consequences of a visit from the fish and game department. To this list of items I won't sell, I would also like to add any taxidermy. Before deciding to sell items of this nature, please check in with your local authorities to learn exactly which types of furs and taxidermy you are allowed to publicly sell in your state.

Chapter 6

....

DO AUCTIONEERS CHEW TOBACCO OR HAVE THEY BECOME SOPHISTICATED?

BEFORE EXPANDING ON THE QUESTION of whether an estate sale or auction is your best option, let's examine two essential questions about auctions: What are auctions? Which type of auction house is best for your personal property?

WHAT ARE AUCTIONS?

Auctions are still the dominant way that personal property is sold or liquidated in America. This is changing especially in our larger cities, where estate sales, yard sales, garage sales, and flea markets are gaining market share. But to ignore auctions and their successful results is a mistake. Auctions are a brilliant sales process by which willing consignors have their personal property placed directly in front of willing buyers, who, if they like the item being offered, will compete against each other until the highest bidder wins the right to purchase the item.

I have often said that the kind of items that should be sent to auction are those that have the best chance of having their values realized and increased through the competitive heat of a bidding process.

I, as an estate liquidator who regularly conducts on-site public estate sales, also offer my clients an auction placement service. Why? Because the values of some of the items I find in homes are so high, they can only be realized through a head-to-head, intensive bidding process.

WHICH TYPE OF AUCTION HOUSE IS BEST FOR YOUR PROPERTY?

Because there are differing styles of auctioning personal property, let's explore what each one of them provides via services or by the prominence of their venues to their clients. Most auction houses, no matter what their economic stature is, whether they are big or small, will generally purport that their auction service is the one to use to sell your personal property to its best advantage. That means most of them think they can get you the highest price for your item. This, though stated in earnest, does not in any way resemble all the facts.

Each auction house has a style that is suited to a specific niche in the auction world. In general, within those niches, each of them has developed a multitude of successful ways to sell your personal property. Some items in your home

This photo of an auctioneer is from *Life* magazine, circa 1938.

will sell for more money if they are presented to international bidders, and other items, because they have modest values, will fare better if they are offered for sale to bidders at a mom and pop auction house by the side of a country road.

The trick is to know the strengths of each auctioning style and consign your personal property accordingly.

THERE ARE FIVE TYPES OF AUCTION HOUSES:

1. International
2. Regional
3. Specialty
4. Real estate and personal property auctions
5. Small mom and pops

INTERNATIONAL AUCTION HOUSES

At the top of the stairs holding their almighty golden gavels stand the absolute rock stars of the auction world. These auctioneers work for the likes of Sotheby's, Christie's, and Bonhams. Their auction gavels routinely hammer

Values for 1920s Chinese Nichol rugs and collectibles like this silver deposit over porcelain coffee set remain strong at estate sales.

down record-breaking prices for paintings by Picasso, violins by Stradivarius, and Qianlong Dynasty porcelains.

On a yearly basis, these three companies alone account for well in excess of $10 billion in worldwide auction sales. Also, it is to auction houses such as these that recently discovered treasures are placed before collectors, museums, and dealers for their preview and purchase.

When someone clearing out an attic discovers old world masterpieces, or when treasure-laden ships are located, or even when the estate of a mogul is settled, phones in these big firms begin to ring.

To get top dollar, and the results that would make even a Midas blush, your high end item will need to be placed before the world's wealthiest and savviest collectors. This is what auction houses like Sotheby's, Christie's and Bonhams are incredibly adept at accomplishing. They have access to a who's who list of buyers with ready stacks of cash that are each demonstrably able to purchase paintings and the like for prices in the millions of dollars.

· ·

You will want to contact a specialist at one of the major auction houses, if you think your item or estate has significant value.

· ·

Don't get me wrong. These companies don't just sell million-dollar paintings, but they do have minimum per-lot values for the types of personal property that they will agree to work with. These per auction lot minimums will vary according to the specific protocols of the auction houses that you are approaching. A good rule of thumb is to figure that the minimum per auction lot value for items offered by the international auction houses is in the neighborhood of $2,500 to $5,000 per auction lot, depending on the category of the item and or the theme of the auction.

So, you will definitely want to attempt to contact a specialist at one of the major auction houses if you think your item or estate has significant value. Just don't expect your first attempt at reaching one of them to be easy. Getting through to the right specialist can seem daunting and these auction houses' websites are like labyrinths. Specialists have assistants who screen calls and you need to speak to them as specifically as you can in order to talk to the specialist. Specialists are busy and there is a lot of auction house prestige riding on their individual decisions. They can be maddeningly difficult to get through to. Try not to take any of this personally. To get a hold of one, you will need to be persistent..

Everyday people are a primary source of treasure: Sure, you say, whatever—these specialists working for the international auction houses are just dealing with the crème de la crème of international jet-setting dealers, museum curators, and wealthy collectors. What would these parties want with the stuff that came out of my house?

My answer to you is one that is not complicated to understand. There are few surprises left to be found in museums. I mean, where would they look? Wealthy collectors already know what is in their collections. It's not likely that they'll suddenly stumble upon and be surprised by the opening of a box or cabinet and having a treasure fall out. Dealers never keep surprises hidden. When they find something of value at one of their client's houses, or if they have a high-value item brought in to them from any number of sources, they'll put them out for sale almost instantly.

The one unknown about hiding places for a treasure to emerge and someday be found is likely to be from your attics, garages and basements. Maybe it's a painting hanging over your grandmother's mantle or an old stained glass lamp that long provided light to read books by in your Aunt Matilda's study. Much of the world's best stuff, items that will sell for astronomical sums of cash coming up for auction today, is coming out of modest estates—from people just like you.

The specialists working for these firms clearly want to hear from you. You just first need to do your homework to be able to know the right descriptive words and phrases to use, when reaching out to speak with one of them, in order to get their undivided attention.

NOTE: It's true that for most of you, the auction galleries in Paris, New York, and London of Sotheby's and Christie's can seem far away. They are. So, my suggestion is for you to look up the phone numbers of one of their many satellite offices generally located in larger U.S. cities.

REGIONAL AUCTION HOUSES

It is likely that the type of auctioneer you'll find yourself approaching will be the one you select from a list of large regional auction houses located somewhere near where you live. Regional auction houses such as Clars in Oakland, California, James Julia in Fairfield, Maine, or Neal's Auction House in New Orleans. These auction houses will typically have company revenues of between $20-$100 million in auction sales every year. That's no small potatoes. Regional auction houses are a force in the auction world and even compete from time to time with the international ones for high end property. This competition keeps both of them on their toes.

The regionals, as I like to call them, more often than not will conduct monthly auctions that are split into one of two categories: estate auctions or fine auctions, or both. In their estate auctions is where you will find more generalized household goods and furnishings, with a sprinkling of moderately

To realize the full value for items like this ivory candle shade and Matilde Poulat sterling Madonna, it's best if you send them to an auction.

high-valued items up for bid. In their fine auctions is where they will place all the best and finest items that were brought to them via various monthly consignments.

These regional auction companies, because they are in competition with the international auction houses, have copied, to the extent they can afford to, the best practices of the international houses. Most of them have qualified staffs that capably assist both buyers and sellers through the entire auction process. In the top tier of their organizations will be experts, appraisers, and specialists.

* *

The one unknown about hiding places for a treasure to emerge and someday be found is likely to be from your attics, garages and basements.

* *

Because these regional companies conduct monthly auctions that are divided into estate goods auctions, as well as fine auctions, they are able to aid and assist their consignors in ways that the large international auction houses simply won't. What I mean by this is that regional auction houses more properly see the symbiosis between your estate's best items and its regular run-of-the-mill household furnishings; that you, as a consignor, have more to deal with then the sale of single high-value items. You have an entire household worth of contents to deal with, and not just a single high-valued item.

They realize that by helping you with what is common and moderately valued in your estate, they stand a better chance, because of the extension of their goodwill and assistance, of also receiving items from your estates that have high or significant value. In this way, they are able to offer you an auction service that is more comprehensive in nature than the international auction houses.

NOTE: The line between what was so special about the international and larger regional auction houses has begun to blur. Regional houses, mostly as a result of the Internet, have begun to level the playing field. Collectors the world over can now find these regional houses, view their online catalogs, and bid via Internet bidding platforms in ways that were not even available to them four or five years ago. So today, the regional houses have a greater reach and draw to their monthly auctions than ever before. This is significant.

SPECIALTY AUCTION HOUSES

Specialty auction houses, as the term suggests, only work within specific areas of antiques and collectibles. For instance, Swann's in New York City

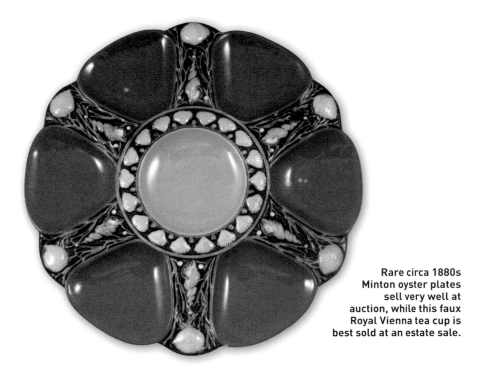

Rare circa 1880s Minton oyster plates sell very well at auction, while this faux Royal Vienna tea cup is best sold at an estate sale.

The costume jewelry Miriam Haskell necklace, at top, has a comparable value to the real pearl and gold bracelet in the photo above.

specializes in auctioning works on paper, so you wouldn't bring them your family's silver; LA Modern in Los Angeles specializes in the sale of high-end mid-century furnishings, so you wouldn't bring them your uncle's antique Georgian dining room table; and Pacific Book Auctions auctions off rare books and manuscripts, so you wouldn't bring them your mom's exquisite porcelain thimble collection.

The good news is that specialty auction houses have, at the very least, the same caliber specialist on their staff that the best of the regional auction houses do, and oftentimes their specialists are many times better than the regional or international houses. Not only that, they also have developed, over the many years of their auction sales, unique relationships with an elite list of collectors the world over who are consistently and reliably in the marketplace for specialized goods. These collectors are willing to bid high for items of particular interest to them.

NOTE: Specialty auction houses like those named above are not the only places that will welcome your specialty collections on consignment for their future auctions. Many of the regional auction houses are also willing to create special single-theme auctions to facilitate the sale of your valuable collections. If you can't reach experts at one of the specialty auction houses or want to avoid shipping expenses and hassles, consider contacting local regional auction houses and asking them how they can create an auction event tailored to your specific situation.

REAL ESTATE AND PERSONAL PROPERTY AUCTIONS

This is my least favorite type of auction, although I know that it's a popular way of auctioning in many parts of the country. In fact, in some parts of the country, it is the primary way that both the selling of real estate and the auctioning of personal property are accomplished. So my negative sentiment about this style of auctioning is not likely to be well received. But if any style of auctioning more typifies the negative images associated with dustbowl or Depression-era auctions— with auctioneers framed on porches sweating and calling out their bids, hammering down penny on the dollar results—this is that type of auction.

My biggest objection to combining the sale of real estate with personal property is that the two seem much at odds with each other. The focus of the auctioneer is too often on the sale of the real estate not the personal property. Their biggest income comes from their sales commission earned from the sale of the house, so that's where they naturally put their attention. Their efforts to auction off the personal property are not nearly as well thought out, marketed, or as robust as the efforts of the mom and pops or regional auction houses.

NOTE: Please do your due diligence. Ask these auctioneers about their track records in regards to the selling of high-value objects found in a home. Have they ever found an item of great value in a home? How did they sell it? In some areas where these auctions take place, homes could be selling in the range of $50,000 to $150,000. A question that occurs to me to ask them is have they ever found an object in a house so valuable that it sold for more than the house itself? Their answer should be yes.

MOM AND POP AUCTION HOUSES

The weekly estate auctions that occur in small towns, rural counties, and even in some of America's larger cities, are the default manner by which the personal property of hundreds of thousands of estates are sold each year.

If you were to view the yearly gross receipts for 10 of these small auction houses and compare them to only one day of the gross receipts for Christie's, Christie's would likely have generated more income on behalf of their clients. But let's not sell these smaller auction houses short; what they are able to accomplish on behalf of their clients on a yearly basis is truly phenomenal. They empty houses quickly. They help people. They get things done.

Their positive efforts for their clients, as well as the commerce they bring to the shopping communities they serve, really can't be measured just in dollars. On a weekly basis, their trucks fan out into the communities where they conduct business to assist families who have no other way to empty out their estates than to use the services of mom and pop auctioneers.

• •

Auctioneers at mom and pop auction houses are becoming more sophisticated, developing relations with non-local buyers, and generating stronger sales results than they have in the past.

• •

Small auction companies have all the personality and character of any family style business. There won't be anything highfalutin' about them. They are as basic, as, you guessed it—apple pie. They're there to get things done because their auctions occur weekly and these companies and their staffs are in constant motion. Most of the people who work for them accomplish and provide daily in unheralded fashion, something the big guys will never be able to. The client hand-holding, the offering of shoulders to cry on, the generation of income to estates—even from what would seem meager and bare to the big guys.

You generally won't find it too hard to get a hold of them and don't be surprised to hear the scattered sounds of traffic and truck noises in the background when their phone is answered. It's as likely as not that you will catch

Lladro figures, unless rare, are best sold at estate sales, but if you have a collection of figural tape measures, you should send them to auction.

these auctioneers in the field on their way to an estate they're working on.

Do the mom and pop auction houses have the in-depth expertise of the international, specialty or regional auction houses? Of course not. But what many of them do have are the right connections. And today it's not uncommon for some of them to have enough acumen to be able to first identify and then evaluate your high-value items, at least to the level of realizing that those items really belong in an international or specialty auction house setting. The best have taken the time needed to establish the right connections. This is definitely something you want to make sure you ask them about.

The Internet has expanded the reach of many mom and pop auction houses. Some of them have begun listing their auctions online through one of several auction listing services, such as liveauctioneers.com and auctionzip.com. This is allowing many of them for the very first time to have a way to reach a buyer base beyond their towns and cities.

When you speak to auctioneers at this level, it is important for you to fully understand their fee structures. Unlike the large auction houses and the regional ones that have tiered fee structures, most of these auction houses will have flat percentage fee structures. Their fees do not rise or fall depending on how much they sell your item for. Their percentage fee is fixed. In this way, they are significantly different than the other auction houses whose fees rise or fall depending on the price the item sells for. These smaller auction houses, when they sell something for a high amount, will still collect their standard fixed rate fee.

NOTE: Mom and pop auctioneers are becoming more sophisticated, developing relations with non-local buyers, and generating stronger sales results than they ever have in the past. Ask them about their past successes. what they found and how they properly sold them.

AUCTIONS OR ESTATE SALES: WHAT'S THE DIFFERENCE?

ESTATE SALES

Many people in less-populated areas of the country are just beginning to hear about estate sales, that they are great places to shop for antiques and collectibles or are profitable ways of liquidating their inherited personal property.

The estate sales industry is growing, largely as a result of estate lawyers, real estate agents, professional organizers, senior citizens relocation consultants, and the like, who have begun to use these services instead of those offered by auction houses. There are many reasons for this, but it mostly comes down to sales results. Estate sales, when conducted in the most professional of manners, oftentimes exceeds even the results of some of the regional auction houses. And more often than any mom and pop auctioneer will ever care to admit, in-house estate sales will exceed their abilities and generate even greater revenue streams.

If you are in the position of having to sell your personal property, whether as a result of inheritance or some other reason, you should most definitely check out the websites of the estate liquidators in your area.

ESTATE SALES SERVICES PROS AND CONS

● PROS:

1. There are no auction house moving costs.
2. They don't charge photo or buy-back fees, and their insurance is included.
3. All items can be individually priced. There are no auction box lot strategies.
4. Low and medium value items often sell for higher prices, than at auctions.
5. The best companies use more than just an estate sale to sell personal property.
6. Commissions and other fees are generally lower.
7. Estate sales are two- or three-day sales events so more buyers can attend.
8. Furnishings can be purchased from a staged home setting, not a warehouse.
9. Prices are fixed and all items are marked.
10. Estate liquidators use many more advertising and marketing strategies.

● CONS:

1. There will be strangers in the decedent's house.
2. Not all estate liquidators are properly insured.
3. Estate sales by themselves are not the best place to sell high-value items.
4. Some companies see themselves as "liquidators," rather than value maximizers.
5. Haggling at estate sales lowers the sold prices.

AUCTION HOUSE SERVICES PROS AND CONS

You can find auction houses all over the country, from out-of-the-way farm auctions to high-end big-city antiques auctions. In many parts of the country, there is simply no other way to liquidate personal property than at an auction.

● PROS:

1. Small town and rural auction houses have strong and loyal buyers.
2. For high-value single items and estates, there is no better sales venue.

3. In small towns and rural areas, auctions are sometimes your only option.
4. House contents can be removed promptly, allowing for quick real estate sales.
5. When valuable items are found, auction houses have access to world markets.
6. Auction houses that post online catalogs generate greater collector interest.
7. Competitive bidding creates an imperative: buyers must bid higher or lose the item.

These contemporary Limoges boxes will sell well at an estate sale; if they were antique, we'd send them to an auction.

8. Large auction houses have specialists with access to important databases.
9. Your item can be consigned with a sale price reserve.
10. Auction houses are located all over the country, even in rural areas.

CONS:

1. Auction houses sell items on a lot-by-lot basis. This means any single item consigned to them is sold to the highest bidder willing to bid at a single point in time. Five minutes before this time, the object is not for sale, and five minutes after this point, the object has been sold or it has been passed. This contrasts sharply with items that are offered at an estate sale in that those items are available for sale on a first-come first-served basis for the duration of a three-day estate sale. There are many who prefer the estate sale way of shopping to the atmosphere and style of an auction.

This Bradley and Hubbard lamp base with its Quezal glass shades will sell at either an estate sale or auction.

THE THREE-TIERED APPROACH

To successfully liquidate an estate's personal property, I recommend the adoption of a three-tiered sales and marketing strategy.

1. Find an advocate.

2. Consign your highest value items to the largest international, specialty, or regional auction houses in your area.

3. Engage the services of an estate liquidation company to sell your estate's low, medium, and medium high value items at an estate sale.

FIND AN ADVOCATE: As I have written in many other places in this book, find an advocate in someone who will make your goals their own, someone who will work for you and has experience. This may be a certified appraiser, a close friend in the antiques business, or an estate liquidator. Emptying out a house and discovering or understanding what has true value is not an easy job. Professionals have spent lifetimes gathering the information necessary to do this right. Doing this yourself is not advised.

CONSIGN HIGHEST VALUE ITEMS TO AUCTION: Once you have retained the services of an expert, they can begin the process of identifying your estate's best items. It is only after this identification process that you can begin to decide whether or not any of your items rise to the value profiles necessary for them to be sold successfully at an auction. Which auction house, whether your item should go to an international auction house, specialty auction house, or regional auction house is determined by your objects' value profiles. Ask whoever you have retained as an advocate or expert many questions about their reasoning for why they suggest that one object goes to one kind of auction house, and not to another. If you prefer to use the services of a local auctioneer, make sure to ask them what special sales tactics they use when selling very high end or valuable items.

ENGAGE AN ESTATE LIQUIDATOR: Carefully read Chapter 12, How to Interview an Estate Liquidator. Their answers to the questions that I pose in that chapter will reveal to you whether you have an estate liquidator who sees their primary role as one of maximizing the value of the personal property in your estate via multiple sales channels, or one that sees themselves as a liquidator. Many estate liquidators are starting to adopt a multi-tiered approach to the sale of personal property. They are actively using the services of international, specialty and regional auction houses to sell items to their best advantage, and then they are conducting in-house estate sales in order to sell the rest of their clients' household contents. They are one-stop shop personal property asset maximizers.

Ideally, the professional estate liquidator to look for is someone who has a finely honed talent for discovering and properly identifying your home's best objects, as well as having the skills necessary of placing your estate's highest- valued items in the right auction.

2. Because auctions sell all items found in a home during a one- or two-day sale, they use "box lots" in order to move large volumes of personal property. When items are combined and offered for sale in box lots, the opportunity to sell those items individually is lost. This tends to dilute the prices your individual items will sell for.
3. The entire auction sales process can drag on for many months.
4. Mom and pop auction houses often lack the necessary expertise to properly identify and or sell high-value items.
5. Large international auction houses place high per-lot value thresholds on items they will accept for consignments. They are only interested in the best of the best.
6. Specialty auction houses have by necessity long consignment-to-auction-date cycles. In other words, it may take four to six months for your consigned items to even come up for sale.
7. Regional auction houses sometimes make the mistake of thinking their auction house is the right place to sell items of the highest value. There are many stories of pickers buying items from regional auction houses, and then consigning them for large profits to the international auction houses.
8. Small auction houses that specialize in combining the auctioning of personal property with real estate are too often focused on the fees they can collect from auctioning the real estate.

ESTATE SALES AND AUCTIONS ARE BOTH VIABLE STRATEGIES

There really is no one size fits all approach to selling all the contents of your family's home. I favor a strategy of combining the best of the services of an estate liquidator with the best of the services of highly qualified auctioneers. But many of your best alternatives will be dependent on where you live. Some areas of the country have few if any estate liquidators who conduct on-site estate sales. Other parts of the country have only mom and pop auctioneers or auctioneers who combine the sale of the personal property with the auctioning of real estate. The regional auction houses can seem remote to you if they are located any further than 50 or 60 miles away.

So you're going to have to do the best you can. Using this book and engaging the services of the most qualified professionals that you can find is your best chance at getting great results.

Chapter 7

WAS YOUR MOM A HOARDER OR COLLECTOR?

HERE'S A QUESTION: What's the difference between what a hoarder hoards and a collector collects? Answer: None. It's a matter of perspective. I'd say both are collectors. The biggest difference between these two types of people is in the way we ascribe a financial value to the stuff a collector collects and the way we subtract an emotional stability value from a person who hoards. In fact, there could be many similarities between the emotional reasons these two groups collect.

A hoarder house is as fascinating and interesting to us as a perplexing riddle. Who lives in that house? Where did they get all that stuff? Why do they hoard? We read about them in newspapers, and watch with a perverse sense of horror as stories about them unfold on TV. And we think we are not like them. We would never do that to ourselves and let our lives get so out of control. We have judgments about hoarders—only bad people do that, only dirty people, people who weren't raised right, or people with mental illnesses. Only people with flawed psychologies hoard. Who else would choose to surround themselves with piles of useless junk?

It is human nature to judge, but your judgments about the actions of the hoarder who may be in your life is probably not going to be of much help to you, especially if the hoarder in question is your mom, dad, or some other family member. For you, if having a hoarder to contend with is the position you find yourself in, it is far more useful to see that you are dealing with a loved one who is afflicted with a behavior that they themselves do not completely comprehend.

· ·

Hoarding is the gathering, or collecting, instinct gone haywire.

· ·

Recognizing a hoarder outside of their home is not all that easy because they'll look just like you or me. They are people, after all, not crazies. They may be the people you're meeting for dinner, for a drink after work, or the guy sitting at the next table in a cafe. They could be members of your prayer group, reading group, or your workout buddy at the gym. These are people who may be highly functioning and perfectly normal in every other area of their lives. It's only at home where they cache and pile, store and hoard—where the secret shame or embarrassment caused by their hoarding plays out.

When you visit your mom or dad or some other family member and you have to speak to them through the crack of their barely opened front door and they won't let you in, this may be your first clue that they are hoarding. This goes for your elderly or eclectic neighbors, who, when you check in on their welfare, you note the strong smells of too many animals, or of mold and decay wafting up and through the slight opening of their front doors.

GATHERING IS INSTINCTUAL; HOARDING IS EMOTIONAL

It's interesting to me how many people don't know that they have a hoarder in the family, preferring to think that it happens to other people and their families, not theirs. I am definitely not an expert in the psychological underpinnings of hoarding, nor am I an expert in all of the terminology of hoarding, but I am an expert in how to deal with the stuff that's been hoarded. Because I have been in so many homes over the years, and a few of them were true blue classic hoarder homes, I have developed some layman's thoughts about the subject.

Gathering is different from hoarding in that it is a defensive strategy or practice that is designed to protect one from a foreseeable future potentiality. Hoarding is more like a divided defense against itself. The more one hoards, the less one is able to prepare for future potentialities.

We've been gatherers as a species since time immemorial. But no caveman would ever have thought to gather so much that they could not have run with all of their possessions if circumstances had dictated such action. By modern standards, a hoarder is a person who has gathered so much to themselves that they cannot easily navigate through it or move it should the time come.

Hoarding is the gathering, or collecting, instinct gone haywire. We know that we are supposed to save up for a rainy day and there's nothing even remotely mistaken about the practices of stocking up or being prepared. Having enough to be self-sufficient, in cases of emergency or natural disaster, is just plain sensible. There are many rational reasons that we acquire things, and save or store them for the one day they will be useful.

The most often cited counterpart for this instinct in us, one that we refer to in casual conversations with each other is our comparison of our gathering nature with that of a squirrel: we "squirrel things away." This is all perfectly acceptable to our families, neighbors, and society as a whole.

People who hoard know they are gathering differently than you and I do. They know that they are at the effect of something they cannot fully control, never mind explain. They know the eyes of the world are judging them and that there are whispers rising up out of the clusters of their families. They know that in relation to stuff, they are different than other people. They feel shame. Hoarding still feels better to them than not hoarding, though. They feel safer by having lots of stuff, then by the idea that freedom could come from an

Try not to assume: What may look like piles of junk or heaps of trash could be the hiding place of something very valuable.

absence of it. You, as a friend or family member, can know the truth of their struggles and how much safer they feel when they are surrounded by all that stuff, by their reaction if you were ever so bold as to threaten to take any of it away. That is when you will see their fear rear its terrified head.

KINDS OF HOARDING

Before describing one of the "hoarder houses" my crew and I worked in, I want to state again that my comments about hoarding and my descriptions of the homes where they live are based on my experience. They are not based on a thorough and rigorous research of the technical and psychological behavior of hoarding. Because I am not a trained behaviorist or psychiatrist, my observations are anecdotal.

THREE HOARDING STYLES

1. Junk pile hoarders.
2. QVC and online shopping hoarders.
3. Collector hoarders.

If you find yourself in the situation of having to deal with the estate of a hoarder while they are still alive, my recommendation is that you seek out the services of professionals who specialize in working with people suffering from hoarding behavior.

JUNK PILE HOARDERS

Junk pile hoarders will mishmash, tumble, and stack just about anything they have into indiscriminate piles. There will be no seeming rhyme nor reason or even patterns to their hoarding style, at least to you. When you excavate through the mass of it, you will find that the old has been mixed with the new, and that the useful has been mixed in with the broken.

I have never been certain whether or not this style of hoarding comes out

CAUTIONARY TIP: It is while in the home of a junk pile hoarder that you as an executor will need to be at your best and most attentive. Until you have done a thorough search through each and every pile and sorted your way through every room, you won't truly know what is in their house. If your hoarder has been gathering for decades, there is no telling what items of value may be buried underneath the detritus of years. Your brightest, most entertained solution to the problem of what to do with that mountain of stuff will be to call a hauler and have them throw it all away. Please remember before you do something so rash that some of my most spectacular and valuable discoveries have come from beneath what was buried in a junk pile hoarder house.

of the conviction by the hoarder that one day these items may become useful or if it arises out of some other strategy. To navigate through their homes, you will have to walk through its rooms on the narrowest of paths between stacks of boxes, newspapers, and old clothing piled high—sometimes even to the ceiling.

QVC AND ONLINE SHOPPING HOARDERS

When I first started in the estate liquidation business, it was before there was much activity on the Internet and also before TV stations like the Home Shopping Network had established themselves so firmly in the marketplace. In those days, I would frequently encounter the estates of people, mostly elderly, who had shopped excessively, buying every new fascinating gadget they could via mail order catalogs or from ads in magazines—things like limited edition plates, figurines, commemorative coins, and figural bottles.

The people who bought this stuff believed the advertised hype that the items they were purchasing, because they were from limited productions, had values that would increase over time. These items always came with authenticating documents and certificates that these buyers were always careful to keep with the limited edition items they had purchased. They did this because the lore or myth about limited edition items is that without the documents or certificates, the item becomes almost worthless. None of these limited edition items had any use, other than as object of so-called collectability.

In some people, the impulse to buy these kinds of objects became highly obsessive and I have been in homes where closets, pantries, and sometimes whole rooms were filled with this sort of property. Sadly, almost none of this stuff, although it can be sold for moderate amounts at estate sales or yard sales, has no high value.

Today because of the Internet and the huge success of TV shopping channels, the elderly or those who might be termed shut-ins have access to a dizzying array of products. They buy because they think they are getting a great deal, but in fact most of what they are buying has nowhere near the value of

CAUTIONARY TIP: The majority of the limited edition plates, bowls, figurines, bottles and so on that you find in these kinds of homes will have little value. Although there are what I call sleepers within these categories—limited edition items that still have high collector value— getting that value may prove to be difficult. Also there are a number of limited-edition items produced that were made from gold and silver, so great care should be given to examining with a loupe all items of jewelry. It doesn't take many gold rings or items of sterling silver found amongst the costume jewelry for this effort to have been worth your while.

what they paid, and when finally sold as used goods at an estate sale or yard sale, sell for pennies on the dollar.

I speculate that people like those I've described really have a two-tiered behavior they are dealing with. On the one hand, their hoarding is to obsessively keep and not let go of anything, and on the other hand, it is an addictive impulse to acquire things that they hope will increase in value. These two impulses are sustained by their online and TV shopping habits.

COLLECTOR HOARDERS

While speaking with my wife, Valetta, about the subject of hoarding, she said, "We're hoarders." And before I could really think about it, I blurted out in classic hoarder style, "We're not hoarders. The stuff we've collected is valuable."

For a collector hoarder, there is a difference between the items they collect and what junk pile hoarders and on-line shopping hoarders collect. Collector hoarders collect items that have historical and financial value. And the collecting world backs their idea of what's valuable by sustaining an entire marketplace that daily trades in the multitude of items that collectors collect. So what your collector hoarder has been stashing away may have a high dollar value. The added benefit to the person who has to go through a collector's hoard is that most of what is there can actually be looked up, have values ascribed, and be easily sold when the time comes.

CAUTIONARY TIP: What you find in a collector hoarder's house, unless their collecting habits were narrow and specific to one or two categories of collectibles, will be spread out over many categories of antiques and collectibles. In either case, even though their houses may look like big junk piles to you, you should make every effort to engage the services of a professional to assist you in ascertaining what these items are, as well as what their proper value may be. In this type of home more than in others, you need to stay patient and calm and gather as much information as you can.

AN ESTATE SALE OF A HOARDER

Lest you think hoarding only occurs out in the country on debris-laden land owned by half deranged old coots carrying shotguns, or at the edge of your town in its marginalized or poor neighborhoods, think again. Hoarding is a behavioral phenomenon that knows no social, economic, or educational boundary; in other words, this behavior can afflict people no matter if they are rich or poor, educated or uneducated.

Messes like this are common in a hoarder home.

Whenever the subject of hoarding comes up, I eventually get to thinking about the project we did on Colon Avenue in San Francisco. This house is in a neighborhood sandwiched between City College and the upscale and wealthy St. Francis Woods. It was a good neighborhood, with strong working-class to upper-middle-class residents. Pride of ownership was evident everywhere— freshly painted stucco and wood framed homes, manicured lawns and gardens, and newer cars parked in most driveways.

From the outside, this hoarder house fit right in. The inside, though, was an entirely different matter. If you had been their neighbor, it would seem unbeknownst to you that a secret family had been living next door to you, quietly going about the business of hoarding for years entirely under the radar of your scrutiny.

••

Hoarding is a behavioral phenomenon that knows no social, economic, or educational boundary. This behavior can afflict people no matter if they are rich or poor, educated or uneducated.

••

A lot of people in the estate liquidation business won't take on a hoarder project because they entail much back-breaking work and the promise of a surprise find—something worth a great deal that would make their Herculean efforts worth it all—often is just a hope that does not always come to fruition. This is an understandable business decision and it is not a lack of ethics; it is the liquidator knowing the limits of their stamina and that of their staff. To call it a Herculean task doesn't adequately describe the planning, many staff hours, and debris removal logistics involved to get through this type of project.

To call it an enormous undertaking is to belittle the undertaking. A better way to describe getting through a hoarder house project like Colon Avenue is to liken it to a fantasy experience of a bucking bull ride, where the rider is able to stay astride the bull through the wildest ride of that bull's life, and then somehow, as if by the act itself, the rider is able to calm and make friends with the bull. The act of getting through a hoarder house will feel like you are having to tame a great and snarling beast; one like that bull who might rather stay wild.

To do the job right means that someone has to go through every single last item in the house. Every single one. Mixed up in the behavior of hoarding can be many small acts of hiding. I have had the experience of finding each of these: money stashed between layers of newspaper, loaded firearms in a dirty clothes hamper, important financial documents in the linen closet. Stuff like this has happened to me so many times, I expect them to happen. In a typical non-hoarder house, there may be as many as 1,000 to 2,000 items. But in a house like the one on Colon Avenue, you can multiply that by 10. If you try to get through 10,000 to 20,000 items by yourself, without the tender mercies of qualified people to help you, you may go mad.

Once we were able to push past the pile partially blocking the front door and get it opened and stand in the entryway, what we beheld was surreal and incredible. Here was a house oppressed by too many things: partially unpacked new product boxes jumbled together with heaps of clothing, old and broken furniture, books, records, and a bicycle or two. These were in the entry and by site line of the entry in the dining room. Turning to my right, I saw tables piled high, boxes, rolled up carpets and matting, broken clocks, pictures hung askew, and tumbles of clothing, and underneath it all, a fairly decent but out of tune Baldwin Spinet Piano; this was the living room. In order to get from the front door to the back bedrooms, we set up a human assembly line and passed back a long train of filled garbage bags.

• •

If you try to get through 10,000 to 20,000 items by yourself, without the tender mercies of qualified people to help you, you may go mad.

• •

I like a house that has the potential for a valuable surprise, it's what we in the business are constantly on the lookout for and it's part of our job description—finding and retrieving of the unknown. So it's a huge process of discovery to locate treasure. Please do not make the mistake of thinking that your hoarder house does not have the potential of having hidden within it items of value. That could be a costly error. Instead, hold that the house might have one, that it's within the realm of possibility, that it's best that you look for them, and not assume there are none. Be diligent, take your time, and work yourself through the process methodically.

Even as a professional, it is hard for me to do as I suggest to you, so I don't make my suggestions to you of being diligent, taking your time, and working your way through the process lightly. Going through a hoarder house and dealing with the 10,000 things you find in them is difficult and challenging to the extreme.

I can't adequately describe the magnitude of the amount of stuff that was in this house in any way that would paint its picture big enough to you. What may be easier for me to describe is how I think the emotional and psychological

Part of the bonanza that made our Herculean task of cleaning out a hoarder home worth the effort.

An executor asked us to find these savings bonds, and we did, but only by going through a house piece by piece.

effort it took on the part of my staff and myself must be similar to the emotional and psychological experiences that the family which owned this house went through. It was daunting, scary, unending, and confusing. And like I said, we're the professionals.

If the upstairs rooms in this house can be described as having been jam packed, then the basement and garage can only be described as being double jam packed—an unending ceaseless ramble and chaos of stuff. There were only one or two narrow winding paths through the garage. The rest of the space was as densely packed as a sold-out stadium during a rock concert. The one thing my crew and I were grateful for, though, was that in this particular hoarder's house, for some unknown reason, this family never stored perishable foodstuffs. I can't tell you how much of a relief that was.

INERTIA

The overwhelming feelings my crew and I experienced while in this house, more so than in others we have done, was a sense of weight, of being stuck, and the dread of thinking that this whole effort was without end and we would never get through it. Later, after the whole process was over, I came to understand that we, as a crew, were having to fight through the inertia that the family themselves had attempted to fight through.

Throughout the house, no matter if we were in the bedroom, living room, dining room, or the garage, we kept finding opened but unused boxes of extra-large garbage bags. They were everywhere. Typically they would be opened and have one or two bags removed from the box. It was as if someone in the family had finally mustered up the courage to start the sorting process and get the house cleared out before deciding that it was just too overwhelming of a task and then quit. After a while, that box would get covered up with stuff, so that the next time that anybody in the family had the bright idea to clean up the house, they wouldn't know where they had put the last box of garbage bags. I'm quite certain that we found as many as thirty to forty boxes of opened but unused garbage bags buried between multiple layers of debris.

What was in that house was the stuff they had inherited from relatives. When mom passed, they boxed up all her stuff and put it in the basement. There were two daughters who went away to college and when they were finished with school, they sent boxes of textbooks along with all of their college papers back home to dad, who stored them. At least one of the daughters raised a family and I think her family moved around a lot, maybe into smaller and smaller spaces, and then all of her family's extra possessions, things she didn't want to part with yet, went to dad's house.

Someone in the family got the ambition sometime in the past to go into the printing business, so they bought a two-ton Goss Printing Press. I am not sure if they ever printed much with it, but somehow it also got stored in the garage, where other family members seeing a fresh empty surface, promptly began using the printing press as a storage platform.

The downstairs room at one time must have functioned as dad's office, and on its shelf-lined walls were the hundreds of books he had ordered through the

It was as if the entire house had become a holding place for the wants, desires, and hopes of the family. No one knew how to act in any effective way to get rid of anything.

mail. Most of these, because he had never opened them, were still in their original cardboard packaging. The desk and the floor soon followed suit as storage places for dad's stuff, until the whole of the room was filled beyond capacity.

It was as if the entire house had become a holding place for the wants, desires, and hopes of the family. No one knew how to act in any effective way to get rid of anything.

My four-person crew worked steadily for weeks in this house, bagging up hundreds of contractor-size plastic garbage bags and dumping them into forty yard debris boxes that we had delivered. We filled six of these to overflowing capacity before being finished with the sorting process. But as I've cautioned elsewhere in this book, we took our time, we never became manic or frenzied,

Even this heavy and archaic two-ton Goss printing press has a customer or collector who wants to buy it.

You can get through this: empty a house, earn income for an estate, and preserve your sanity. Get help!

and we made sure that we looked through each and every thing that there was.

Then one day, after all of the effort and the respect and honor that we had shown, our patience and diligence paid off. Down in the mold and dust of the dimly lit garage beneath piles of sheets and old blankets was a metal chest, heavy and locked. We had to break into it and as we did, coins came spilling out like a Las Vegas slot machine; our lucky day to be sure. The family had no clue they were there nor which family member stashed this chest away, though I suspect it was the dad. A month or so before I got to this house, a brother in the family had gone through it and took anything of value before the other family members could, including the guns, but he missed this chest. The family of this estate earned an unexpected $20,000 that day from a mixture of old silver coins and regular currency.

So when I say that you never know what might be underneath the hoarder pile, believe me, none of us do, until we carefully take a peek and look.

CHECK THE INTERNET FOR THESE RESOURCES:

International OCD Foundation: www.ocfoundation.org

Children of Hoarders: www.childrenofhoarders.com

Clutterers Anonymous: sites.google.com/site/clutterersanonymous

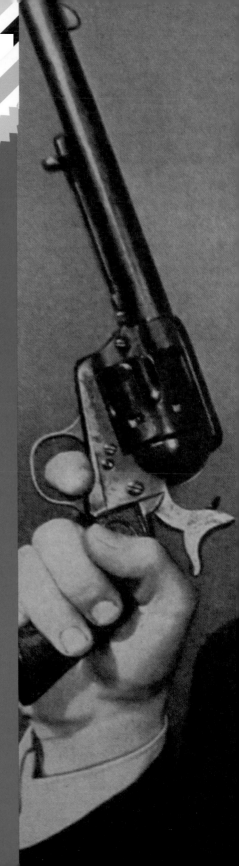

Chapter 8

MY UNCLE SAYS IT'S LEGAL FOR HIM TO KEEP GRANDPA'S GUNS

NO MATTER IF YOU THINK gun ownership is right or wrong, it is a fact that many estates contain firearms, and it is especially important for you as the trustee or executor of such an estate to discover what local laws apply to the disbursement or sale of firearms. Do this before allowing yourself to be pressured into making uninformed decisions that you may regret later. To do other than this is to possibly endanger the estate, or worse, a human life.

SHOULD I GIVE GRANDPA'S GUNS TO FAMILY MEMBERS?

This is the kind of thing that happens more often than not—the impulse to casually give grandpa's guns to various people in families where there has been an active participation between the grandfather and his family in the use of firearms, whether for hunting or target practice. It seems perfectly natural that grandfather's firearms would be passed down through the family.

This might be the right thing to do, but it could also turn into a terrible and costly mistake.

Whether you live in Manhattan, Scranton, or Detroit, firearms are a fact of life in America. People own guns. You as an executor have to deal with personal property, including firearms. You may be anti-gun or pro-gun, but your politics about them really don't have a place here. Unless you are given specific direction via the will to ignore the value of the guns, and decide to give them to family members as you see fit or have them destroyed, you will still need to treat them as one of the estate's assets.

There are tens of millions of firearms in America, so finding one, two, or even a hundred of them in an estate would not be altogether surprising.

You may find firearms safely stored all in one place or hidden all through a house.

What might surprise you is that some of these firearms are extraordinarily valuable. Do you think you're the right person to know whether the firearms in the estate that you are working within are valuable? And what about all of the laws relating to firearms, including municipal, state and federal? Do you know what the law is in your specific area concerning the transfer or sale of firearms?

But you ask, "Who will know if I give the firearms to family members outside of the proper legal channels?" The answer is maybe no one. But what if, heaven forbid, in the future, an heir used a firearm from your grandfather's estate in an inappropriate manner and this firearm was somehow traced back to the estate?

If there is no paper trail, no demonstrable chain of ownership transfer, could the estate be held liable? Could you as the executor, because you did not follow proper protocols, be arrested and jailed? Would there be economic consequences after the fact that would endanger your family's assets? What if later, one of the firearms that you did not have properly appraised was found to be valuable? Is it possible in a case like that that other family members would feel cheated enough to come after you or the estate? Maybe.

Do you really need headaches like those described above? If there are firearms in the home and you are responsible for them because of your role as an executor, do your research, contact your attorney, develop and stick to a plan, and thoroughly document your actions.

THE FAMILY WANTS THE GUNS

If you handle the disbursement of firearms to various family members improperly, or outside of the laws of your local jurisdictions, you may be opening yourself up to an explosive powder keg of problems.

This is no laughing matter. In estates across the country, firearms are being transferred from one family member to another in ways that may not be legal, and because the transfer was not done properly, the estates from whence those improperly disbursed firearms came may find themselves encumbered by any number of consequences and liabilities.

The most likely estate where this sort of scenario occurs is in the estate of a hunter—someone who, over the course of their long life, had many practical reasons to acquire their firearms. Let's say your grandfather hunted over the course of a fifty-year period and in that time he was able to acquire a variety of firearms, each one specific to a certain species of animal or hunting style. Or maybe he was a marksman, each week going out to the range for target practice. In either case, they may have acquired as many as 10 or 15 different firearms, sometimes many more.

In a family where there is a culture of hunting or firearms collecting or both, often these activities by the grandfather will become family activities. In other words, a grandfather, by his hunting or sharp-shooting activities, will have encouraged these activities in his children, and by extension, to his grandchildren. It is not outside the realm of possibility that each of his family members will feel that "grandpa's guns" belong to them.

> **DO NOT SELL OR DISBURSE FIREARMS UNTIL YOU:**
> 1. Unload all firearms.
> 2. Check local laws.
> 3. Determine values.
> 4. Formalize a detailed plan

And there's nothing wrong with this. These firearms do belong to the family, and if it was the grandfather's direct wishes that his firearms should be passed down to his descendants, or if because there is no written will, it has been decided by the executor that it is okay to pass them down to other family members, That's fine. I only have four suggestions:

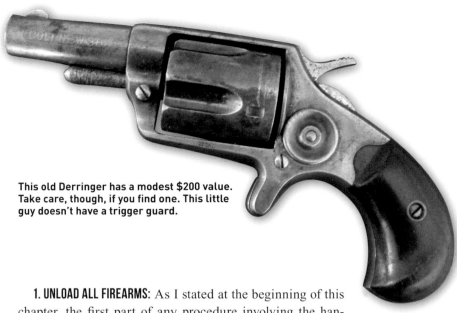

This old Derringer has a modest $200 value. Take care, though, if you find one. This little guy doesn't have a trigger guard.

1. UNLOAD ALL FIREARMS: As I stated at the beginning of this chapter, the first part of any procedure involving the handling of inherited firearms is that each one of them needs to be checked in order to make sure they are unloaded. If you have never handled a firearm, or for any reason have reservations about how to safely handle them, then you must know that you are not the right person for the job. Seek the assistance of a trusted family member who has familiarity with how to safely handle firearms, or employ the services of a local gunsmith.

If you use a gunsmith, then you need to know that once they have seen the firearms collection, they might attempt to buy a few of them; please resist this. Do not sell firearms to anybody until you have accomplished each of the four tasks on the four-point checklist.

When I state that you should get the assistance of a trusted family member or a gunsmith to make sure your firearms are unloaded, I mean that. If you find a cache of firearms or even a single weapon in an estate that you are an executor for, this is not the time to self teach your way through the process of making sure that they are unloaded. Firearms are not casual. Sometimes there is an unknown about bullet in the chamber, other times the manner of unclipping a clip of ammo is tricky. Ammo left too long in a chamber or magazine can also become corroded enough to get stuck. Do not attempt to pry these bullets out—the consequences for such rash action can be deadly.

It is only after you have made sure that all firearms are unloaded and safe to be handled that you can even contemplate scheduling any future meeting to allow other family members to look them over. Make sure you protect the physical well being of your family by being extraordinarily cautious, and by insisting that they be as well. Have doubts? Get help!

A FIREARM WITH HIDDEN VALUE*

In 2008, John McBride, 80, a forester in Libby, Montana, discussed with his wife the best ways their estate could be divided up for their family and who should get what after they passed on. They wanted to make sure everything was fair and that their children would feel they had each received an equal share of their lifetime's worth of accumulations. This is not an unusual conversation amongst the aged. Parents, more often than not, want the best for their kids, for each of them to know that they each had occupied a special but equal place in their hearts. They will go to great pains to figure out just how to do this, but the "how" is never easy.

They did not live in a big fancy house. They were not rich. They were of relatively modest means and not showy or ostentatious; they were just average folks. They lived in a small town of about 2,600 people, far from the city lifestyles of Butte or Billings, Montana. They had one heirloom that was worth a great deal of money. Like a lot of things that have great financial value, this piece not only represented a kind of mythological legend within the family, but it also was a piece of American history. McBride worried about it a bit, and he and his wife had many conversations about what to do with this iconic piece. They began planning. They knew that it had to be sold in order for them to reach their goals, and once sold, they wanted to use the proceeds to buy a large piece of land they would leave to their family.

All of McBride's life, he had collected antique and vintage firearms and always appreciated their history. There are, broadly speaking, two types of firearms collectors: one who collects to preserve them in much the same way a specialist curating a collection for a museum does, and those who collect firearms because they are interested in using them for hunting or target practice. This latter group is sometimes called "shooters."

McBride belonged to the shooters group and used his guns for target practice and would take them out into the field to pop off a few rounds. Now, this is no casual interest. It takes time and more than a passing interest in the entire process of loading, firing, and reloading again. And there is a big drawback to this as well: If you are a shooter of antique or vintage firearms or an old-style hunter who uses them regularly, then with every shot fired, the value of your old gun goes down because of wear and tear. McBride was okay with this, so his collection was not worth a great deal of money.

McBride's great-great uncle had served alongside the Texas Rangers near the conclusion of the Mexican-American war, as well as being an officer from Maryland during the Civil War. At some point, and no one really knows how or when, this uncle acquired a Colt Walker pistol. When this uncle passed away in 1891, it was passed down through the family to a grand niece, who was McBride's mother. The Colt Walker

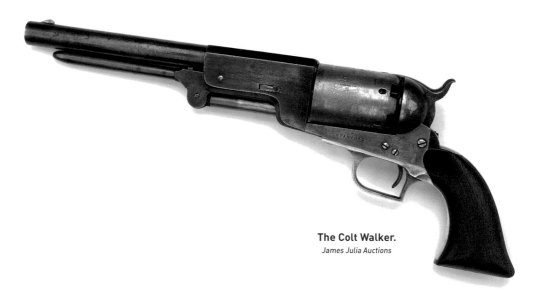

The Colt Walker.
James Julia Auctions

pistol was made circa 1847, so it was an old pistol when McBride first inherited it, and it was in very fine condition—so fine that even in the mid-1940s, he was offered $4,000 for it. Imagine what a family could do with $4,000 back then. McBride knew it was a valuable gun and at various times he showed it to collectors or at a few gun shows and it always generated tons of interest, but it wasn't for sale.

He kept the pistol and never shot it. As a shooter, this was not easy for him to do, but it preserved its value. Now in the sunset of his years and wanting to do the best by his children, McBride and his wife decided to sell the Colt Walker at auction. They contacted James D. Julia of Julia Auctions because James has built quite a reputation as one of the most reputable auctioneers of firearms in America. Somehow, while communicating with Mr. Julia, McBride discovered that James had once worked in the mill near where he worked, and that personal connection, along with Mr. Julia's impressive track record, was enough for the McBrides to make the decision to consign their precious pistol with Julia's.

On Oct. 7, 2008, at the beginning of one of the largest economic meltdowns in our history and a time that you wouldn't expect anybody to be spending copious amounts of money, the Colt Walker sold for an astounding $920,000—a record for the highest price realized at auction for the sale of a single firearm.

*Source: This story is a dramatization based upon an interview that I conducted with James D. Julia, as well as an article that I read in the *Kootenai Valley Record.*

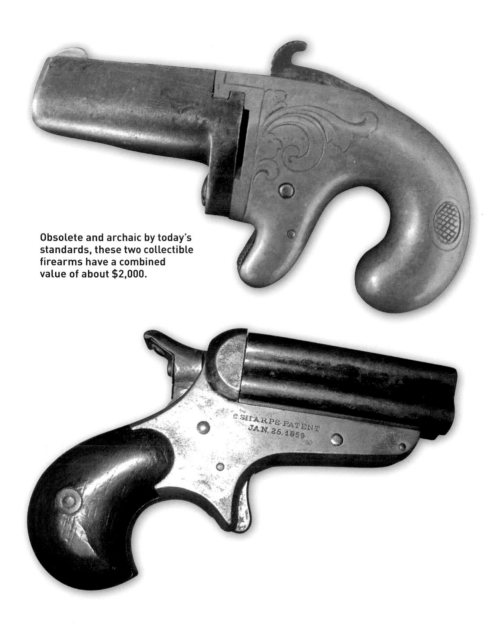

Obsolete and archaic by today's standards, these two collectible firearms have a combined value of about $2,000.

2. CHECK LOCAL LAWS: If you find firearms in an estate, your first contact point for seeking advice about what to legally do with them should be your attorney. Let your attorney know everything that you can about the nature, quantity, and condition of any and all firearms. You want to ask your attorney to please explain in laymen's terms the specifics of the law within your local area concerning firearms sales to dealers or transfer of ownership to family members or any friends of the decedent named in the will.

In most jurisdictions, there are various restrictions against even the own-

If there are firearms in the home and you are responsible for them because of your role as an executor, do your research, contact your attorney, develop and stick to a plan, and thoroughly document your actions.

ership, never mind the sale, of certain classes of firearms. You need to be absolutely sure that none of the firearms in the estate's collection fall under the category of "illegal to own." If they are illegal to own, they are illegal to sell or to give to other family members, so don't do either under any circumstances. A special set of actions are required in order to deal with these illegal firearms. You must follow stringent rules and guidelines. To do otherwise is to open up your estate to grave legal consequences and liabilities. Always check in with your attorney, and if you don't have one, get one!

3. DETERMINE VALUES: Once you have made sure all of grandpa's guns are, in fact, unloaded, and you have received the okay from your attorney, you can begin the process of determining the value of any single firearm or how much the entire collection is worth.

There are many price points for contemporary, vintage, and antiques firearms, which can be worth pocket change or big dough, from a low-valued $50 pistol or rifle to the record-breaking auction results of the $920,000 Colt Walker. Determining how much a firearm is worth is not always easy, so you'll have to do your homework.

If grandpa, or whoever the family's gun collector might have been, was astute enough to keep records about their value, or insightful enough to inform the family about the value, your job may not be so hard. The difficulty to determining the value of firearms is the same as with any other category of antique or collectible. It's the nuances, the pesky details, the little differences between one model gun and another that either adds or subtracts value.

Look for any sort of inventory list the decedent might have compiled, or, if they knew that their collection was valuable, they may have had an appraisal made for insurance purposes. If they compiled their own inventory list or had an appraisal made, then you at least have a head start in the compiling of a list for your own purposes. A note about their inventory list or appraisal document though: It is not a good idea to take those document's ideas about value as fact, rather you want to use them as a guideline. The market changes and shifts almost every day. A high value one day might be a low value the next, and vice versa. At this point, selling or giving any of the firearms to any family members for the values listed in the appraisal or inventory document would be a mistake.

CONSIDER BOTH FINANCIAL AND SENTIMENTAL VALUE

Think. How could the lives of your estate's heirs be changed via the receipt of a large cash infusion from the sale of a few firearms that ultimately proved to be valuable?

When thinking about what to do with firearms, it is important to remember financial value, as well as sentimental value. Maybe you do not have a Colt Walker pistol worth $920,000 in the estate that you represent. No problem, but what are the estate's firearms worth? This is a critical question to answer before ever transferring the ownership of an estate's firearms from the decedent to anyone else named or unnamed by their will.

Resist pressure from family members or anyone else about selling or giving away the guns until you have well established their values.

If you cannot find an appraisal document or an inventory list compiled by the decedent, then you will need to have an inventory list compiled. I do not recommend that you make this list yourself. Determining the make, model, and condition of a single firearm, never mind a collection of them, takes time and expertise and is a job for a professional. Engage the services of a certified appraiser, auctioneer with a proven track record, or a local gunsmith whose ethics are without question. Take time with this and don't commit to the services of any expert without first having interviewed at least three of them.

The best case scenario for you, though, is that you are able to find an appraisal or inventory document somewhere in the house where the firearms are located. If you are able to find such a list, not only will this save the estate money, it will also allow you to quickly forward details about the firearms to your attorney, various dealers, appraisers, and auctioneers.

My sales preference for firearms that are thought to be of high value is to go to other professionals: auction houses that specialize in premier or historical firearms because they know way more than I do. They handle and sell firearms each day, so to protect my clients, I always use the best, most ethical auctioneer I can find who has a proven track record.

But I live in a big city and have access to many local experts. I also use the Internet to identify and research firearms that I find in homes, which gives me a good idea about where and how they should be sold. I can take multiple photos, attach them to inventories I have created, and send it all to auctioneers and appraisers who specialize in the valuation and sale of firearms across the country. You may not have these abilities, or be in the position of having already developed relationships with the right firearms experts. You may not know how to properly document your firearms collection with an inventory list complete with photos. This is why I advise you to find a local expert based on recommendations by people you know to be reliable. You are going to have to pay for this service, but don't trade an expert's services for items that were in the collection; cut these people a check. Contact local gunsmiths, as they will sometimes be interested in this sort of arrangement.

Also ask your attorney for any referrals they may have. Go to your local mom and pop auction houses and discuss with those auctioneers what exactly their experiences and expertise is in bringing firearms into the market. A provable track record is of utmost importance. If you know that you have high-value firearms, and these small auctioneers state that they can sell them for their true value, you need to ask them how exactly they will be able to do so. Small auction houses do not get the same results as specialty auction houses do; if they insist that they can, you may want to take your collection elsewhere.

If you need to rely on the services of a small auction house, the main thing you want to find out is if they know how to get the best of the best in your firearms collection to the better auction houses. They should know how to do this, and if so, then they could be the right auction house for you. Get their references, though, and most definitely check those references.

When you go to the small auction houses or visit one of your local gunsmiths, do not bring the firearms with you. At first, also be a bit secretive about where you live and don't spill the beans too quickly about your collection. Your first visit is a fact-finding mission, so ask a lot of questions and formulate your plans based on their answers.

A .44 Auto Mag pistol from the estate of a big game hunter that we sold via Greg Martin Auctions for $1,500.

This Walther PP, while looking ordinary, is worth $500. Before making disbursement decisions, find out values.

4. FORMALIZE A DETAILED PLAN: Now that you have made sure that all the guns in the estate have been safely unloaded and are locked and stowed away, you have sought the advice of your attorney, and have compiled an inventory list of the firearms that are contained in the estate, you can now formulate a plan. Buy a folder and place into it the following:

- Inventory of all firearms with photographs
- Contact list of experts, auctioneers, and appraisers
- List of people named in will as being beneficiaries of the firearms
- A written action plan for firearms sale or disbursal

A thoroughly detailed and written action plan that has the approval of your attorney, as well as one that contains vital information about the collection, will help you best determine which actions to take, and when, on behalf of the estate. Your plan needs to incorporate within it a time line of which beneficiaries inherits which firearm, as well as details about which auction house is to receive inventory, and the dates the auction house will offer your firearms for sale.

Document in as great detail as you can, each of your actions. If you disperse a firearm to a family member, write it down; give some ammo to the guy next door, write it down; sell firearms to a gunsmith in town, write it down; send the collection of firearms to an auctioneer, write it down. Make sure your document folder contains names, dates, and places.

•••

Determining the make, model, and condition of a single firearm takes time and expertise and is a job for a professional.

•••

FOLLOW YOUR ATTORNEY'S ADVICE

After all, you are paying them, and they know more about the law then you do, so follow their advice. Keep the estate that you represent as free from liability as you possibly can. Have a family member wanting to dispute your plan? Let your attorney know about the family member's concerns, and get back to this family member as soon as you can with your attorney's legal opinion. Work it out with them, but again, remember these are firearms, not trinkets or diamonds—make sure all of your actions are above board, legal, and explainable.

FIREARM SALES FROM AN ESTATE LIQUIDATOR'S PERSPECTIVE

Most estate liquidators, especially ones who run their businesses out of large cities, won't see many firearms in the homes of their clients. This is mostly due to the fact that families have already distributed the firearms to family members or have sold them. This is a good thing because your average estate liquidator is not necessarily the most qualified or educated enough in the law to liquidate firearms properly. This, however, is not the case with all estate liquidators, and there are some who have learned how to do this without the possibility of bringing any negative liability to an estate. It is my guess, though, that most won't know how to do this.

FOUR ESTATES WHERE I DEALT WITH FIREARMS

CASE 1: The first firearm I ever remember finding in an estate was in a city north of San Francisco called Santa Rosa. The firearms were in a white stucco Spanish-style home in one of that city's older neighborhoods. The owners of the home had been in the jewelry business and owned a store in the heart of Santa Rosa's downtown for many years. The elderly woman who had recently passed away had many loaded firearms all around the house. I guess she was nervous. After all, she had been in the jewelry trade her whole life, so maybe she had a stash of diamonds somewhere in the house, which I am sure her family found upon her passing. She liked her security.

We found loaded firearms under her bed, in linen closets, in out-of-the-way storage cabinets. Some of them must of been stored away for a long time because in a few of the pistols, the bullets had become somewhat frozen in their barrels and chambers—bullets left too long in a gun can corrode and get stuck. All in all, it was a dangerous situation and one that required careful handling in order to make sure that each of these firearms had had their corroded bullets safely removed and could be said to be unloaded.

The most surprising thing about finding these approximately ten loaded firearms was that the family had not looked carefully enough through the house to find them. This is also the estate where I relate the story of having found a Bic Pen box with a stack of hundred dollar bills in it (see P. 96). It's crazy and astounding and begs the question of how many people in the situation of having to deal with the personal property of an estate do not look carefully enough through the contents of a home to find the guns and money? Maybe they don't have the time or feel they are too busy with their lives, and so tired and frustrated that they can't be bothered with looking. I'm not sure what was going on. I just know that when it came to the guns in this house, they were not hard to find.

The cautionary note about this is, suppose these firearms had been found by somebody other than a professional who was able to safely unload each of them? What if they had fallen into the wrong hands? What sort of liability would this estate have opened itself up to?

WHAT I DID: Because these particular firearms were each in such poor condition and not collectible, I brought them to a local gunsmith and legally sold them on behalf of this estate.

CASE #2: I did an estate buyout in San Francisco of a ramshackle home filled, for the most part, with modestly valued items. It was close to the beginning of my career as an estate liquidator. While in the garage sorting through the contents that were piled there, literally under some blankets, I found a loaded 32-caliber semi-automatic pistol.

No one had lived in this house for a long time. Neighbors, and possibly other people, must've known that the house was unoccupied. This is the perfect kind of house that might have become a target, please pardon the pun, of a burglary. Imagine if this particular weapon had ended up in the wrong hands. Every day, estate liquidators are handed over the keys to homes all across America, which is fine, we're professionals and we know what we're doing. What is scary and potentially harmful to the estate, though, is that the executor did not go through the home or hire a person to go through it thoroughly enough. They did not make sure that they knew exactly what was in the home before turning over the key.

WHAT I DID: I legally transferred ownership of this weapon to a licensed firearms dealer.

CASE #3: In 2008, I got a call from a woman who was the daughter of a man who collected Colt commemorative pistols. The man was elderly and in poor health, and he had recently suffered a personal tragedy. It seems that while he and his girlfriend were out for a spin on his motorcycle, a bee attacked him, and while physically fending off the bee, he lost control of his motorcycle and crashed. His girlfriend lost her life in that accident. Undoubtedly this tragedy led to depression, which led to him not taking the best care of himself.

The daughter told me about her father's Colt commemorative pistol collection. Most of the time commemoratives or limited edition items are not worth all that much. But in the case of these pistols, they did indeed have value. In fact, the value for them had steadily increased since the first day of their manufacture. To a collector, they would be described as magnificent, stunning even. They were so beautiful that even if you are the kind of person who could not imagine yourself ever owning a firearm, you might make an exception for these. They were that nice.

Part of a six-shot knuckle duster found in a San Francisco estate; even in this poor condition, this has value.

And even though they were replicas, that does not mean that they were in any way inoperable. Each of these Colt commemorative pistols was in every way a fully functioning and operable firearm, and because of this, they each needed to be handled just like you would any other firearm—very carefully.

WHAT I DID: A Colt commemorative pistol, or any other firearm that has col-

This Harrington & Richardson Arms .32 caliber pistol was never an expensive gun and in this condition is useful only as parts to a gunsmith.

lectible or historical value, can only have that value best realized by having it offered and sold at an auction. But these are not the kinds of guns you take down to your local mom and pop auction house. No, these are the types of firearms that you need to take time with, that you need to research, in order to fully understand their value. Once you know what they are, as well as how much they might be worth, then you will know where they should be sold. This was my process: first research them and ascribe a value before making any decisions about where or how to sell them. In this particular case, I sent the whole collection off to a specialty auction house that had the necessary expertise to sell them for the highest price possible. The result of my efforts on behalf of this client was that their 39 pistols sold for a total of $42,000.

CASE #4: Once upon a time, there was a man who lived in San Francisco during the 1989 Loma Prieta earthquake. San Franciscans rocked harder that day then they had at no time since the glory days of rock 'n' roll concerts in Golden Gate Park.

The lights in the Marina District where he lived went out. There was no electricity. Some homes and apartment buildings in his neighborhood were ablaze, a thick collective plume of smoke that could be seen from most parts of the city rose up and stretched into the twilight sky. The only access to information about what was going on in the city of San Francisco that this man had was an AM FM radio that also had a police scanner.

He and his longtime girlfriend listened to many police reports on the scanner about break-ins and other happenings around the city, which to them seemed dangerous. They began from that day forward to fear that a natural disaster could be of such a magnitude that it might lead to anarchy or prolonged periods of civil disobedience. They wanted no part of that scenario and began to research ways to protect themselves and effectively survive a breakdown of civil society, should that ever occur. Innocently enough, they began to acquire firearms and stockpile ammunition. To make a long story short, this man passed away 20 years later, and that's when I received a call from the executor of his estate. In the 20 years that he had collected firearms, he had amassed over a hundred of them, as well as a fair amount of ammunition.

I tell you this story because some of you in the estates that you represent may in fact find such a horde of firearms. I don't know if the estate where you find a stash of firearms will be out in the deep country, a small town, or in a large city. Some of you are going to have to learn a lot in a short time about how to deal with this sort of situation.

WHAT I DID: Of course I first made sure that each and every single firearm in this man's collection was unloaded. I also determined that all of his firearms were legally owned. I did some preliminary research. Once those three things were accomplished, I divided up his collection of firearms into three categories: firearms that I sold to a license firearms dealer; those that I consigned to a regional auction house; and firearms that I consigned to a specialty auction house because of their value.

Read this chapter carefully, employ its strategies,
absolutely consult with an attorney, follow the law,
and you will get through this.

No single book or guide will teach you everything you need to know about the subject of firearms sales and family distributions, so it is important that you combine information from multiple sources about what are the necessary steps to legally sell firearms to others, or how to legally transfer ownership of an estates firearms to various family members. Your attorney can let you know about the law; gunsmiths, auctioneers, and appraisers can let you know about value; with information from each of these sources, when properly combined, you can successfully formulate your best plan of action.

Read this chapter carefully, employ its strategies, absolutely consult with an attorney, follow the law, and you will get through this. It won't be easy, but you will get through it.

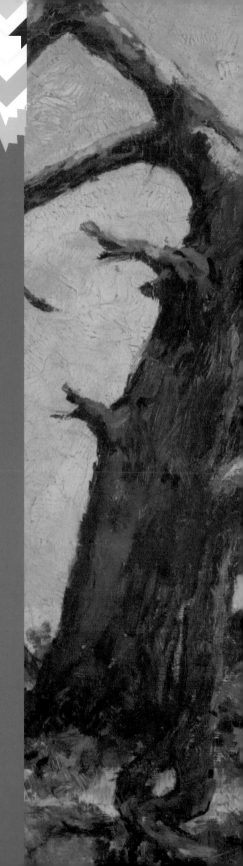

Chapter 9

TWENTY VALUABLE THINGS NOT FOUND IN MANSIONS

ONCE UPON A TIME in a not so far away land, someone close to you, probably a distant family member, acquired something maybe from one of their ancestors or through a purchase they made, never imagining, or maybe knowing all along, that this something had extraordinary value.

As children, most of us saw some movie or read in a book stories about treasures that had been cleverly buried and so secretly hidden away that the person who buried it, wanting to be sure that they would find their way back to the treasure again, drew up a map and placed an X on it.

For me, the X on this map represents the power and mystery of the imagination. If we only had that kind of map and knew what was buried under that X, what resources would we then employ, to book passage on what ship, to get us to which island, knowing that once there, with but a simple shovel and the act of digging, that we would find a trove of what is gleaming and precious.

Every single house has, at the very least, the potential of being a place where you could exercise the imagination of a child and ask yourself the question, If there were treasure buried here, what would it look like and where would it be buried?

To me, an integral part of the concept of treasure, as thought about in connection with the personal property of an estate, is that these are the kinds of items that everyone in a family has seen for years, but not really thought about as a treasurer at all. They were just the things that grandma left you or a colorful gewgaw that your traveling uncle brought back from some distant shore.

These are the kinds of treasures so cleverly hidden, that it reminds me of the Edgar Allen Poe story, "The Purloined Letter," about an object carefully sought after, but not easily found because it had been hidden in "plain sight."

Many treasures do not require a map for you to find them because they are hidden in plain sight. If you are an executor in charge of an estate or a family member who has recently inherited the personal property of someone who has passed away, the only thing that is required of you to find a treasure, should it exist, is that you maintain an open mind and let your curiosity be your guide.

A NOTE ABOUT THIS CHAPTER: Each of the items featured here were found by me personally or were brought to my attention by a member of my incredible staff. They are things I sold for the amounts that I state. Each of these items was found exactly where I state they were found. Where some embellishment to these examples was made was in the descriptions concerning the families where these items were found and sold. My descriptions of the people who were part of these estates reflect my impressions of who they might have actually been, based on the time that I spent in their homes and by the anecdotes told to me.

TWENTY ITEMS SOLD CAN ADD UP TO $1,083,253, AND THAT'S BIG BUCKS

Everyone wants an *I Dream of Jeannie* moment, or to have Elizabeth Montgomery show up in your living room twitching her nose magically until a treasure appears. Most homes have average stuff in them, though, and you need to know that. Treasures are few and far between, but don't despair. The sale of the average everyday stuff in your home, when added up dollar by dollar, can still add up to an impressive amount.

It is not unusual that when everything from a modest estate is sold, the estate can earn an income of as much as $5,000. By an estate liquidator's reckoning, that's not a lot of money, but to you and your co-heirs, this could be a significant amount. It could be used to pay some of the estate's obligations and so on. Try not to get discouraged because you think the house is full of a pile of junk and you have no idea how you are going to get the sale of the stuff to make ends meet. My three greatest personal finds came from junk pile homes, so take care.

Try to imagine that this whole empty-the-house project is an incredible chance for you to learn. When you keep a beginner's attitude, you will be better prepared and open to the possibility of finding a treasure … something unknown to you before you began this process that you can sell for real money.

As I have written elsewhere in this book, don't imagine that you can do this by yourself, though. You will need to find the right people to help you and your first task is to learn who those people are that you should be seeking out for their expert guidance, and then contact them. Expect to be asked to pay for the services of professionals.

1 HOARD OF GOLD AND SILVER COINS SOLD VIA OUR BROKERAGE SERVICE TO A DEALER FOR $357,328

On P. 212, I have written about how I came to work with the client who was in charge of the estate where these coins were found.

When I describe the house as being modest, picture one of the more modest homes in your town, and then put that home in one of your town's poorer neighborhoods. It was in a house like that where these coins were gathered and stored over the course of one man's lifetime.

I never quite got the whole story from the family; the incredibly competent woman I worked with was the man's niece. She was a force of nature and it is largely through her persistent efforts that she was able to secure for her family such a great result for the sale of these coins.

What do you do when you find a large cash treasure and the house is on the edge of a ghetto, and many members of your family are circling the house like hungry and complaining vultures? You do what this young, courageous woman did. She and her father removed the coins out of the home and transported them all to a bank, where they rented 12 large safety deposit boxes to keep them safe. Then she inventoried every single last coin—a Herculean effort for a coin dealer, never mind someone who may never have looked at a single gold coin before then. The third thing she did was to find someone she could trust to act as an agent for their sale, and that is how I came into the picture.

Selling this size of a collection is not exactly easy. I tried a few of the auction houses, but because most of these coins were bullion, they didn't want to handle them. I started to seek out bids from three of the largest metals buyers in northern California, and even I was surprised that there was more than a $100,000 difference between the lowest and highest bid. It definitely pays to get multiple bids.

Once we had the bids in place and our client agreed to their purchase price, we hired an armed guard to ride with me and we drove the coins to the person who had offered us the most amount of money. That day we helped our client and her family sell a giant stash of coins at the very top of the market for $357,328.

MORAL: Secure assets. Make inventories. Find someone you can trust. Always get more than one bid.

2   EDUARD GAERTNER PAINTING SOLD FOR $266,000

I got a call from an elderly woman who lived with her husband in a modest middle-class home in a small town that hugged the northeastern shore of the San Francisco Bay. She told me that she had a few paintings and many items made from sterling silver. She had received a mailer from me many years before while she still lived in the city of San Francisco, and thinking that one day she might need my services, she saved my brochure, which turned out to be lucky for both of us.

She wanted me to buy the paintings and silver on the spot and asked me to make an offer. The thing about making an offer to buy items like this on the spot without being able to do any research is that the person making the offer tends to make a low one because they don't know exactly what they're buying or how much it's really worth. At first she was adamant about wanting to sell her items as a group, and she did not want to consign her stuff. She only wanted to know how much I was willing to pay and that was that.

These coins came from a middle class man's home and were sold by us to SF Gold Buyer.
Fine Estate Liquidation

This Eduard Gaertner painting came from a prototypical little old lady's house and was sold via Michaans Auctions. *Michaan's Auctions, Alameda, CA*

Her silver was easy to make an offer on, but her six or seven small oil paintings were more difficult to value without access to my research resources, so I did what anybody else in that situation would do: I shot blindly and hoped I'd hit her target price.

I can still remember sitting at her dining room table looking at her group of paintings and bits and pieces of silver and her, after hearing my offer, shaking her head and saying no. It was like a movie. She said that my offer was too low. Too low? Did she know what everything was worth? Of course not, but she had a feeling … maybe a sixth sense or something. I explained that it was impossible for anyone to make a qualified offer for her stuff without first doing some research, especially for the paintings. I explained the logic of the consignment process to her and she finally consented.

One of the paintings in that group turned out to be by Eduard Gaertner, an important Berlin painter, and at the end of the auction, it hammered down at $266,000. Not a bad result for a painting found hanging in a small modest home.

In case you think that I was acting in a manner that was not adequate to the task of valuing these paintings out in the field far from a computer, you would be partially right. Another interesting note about this painting was that even the large regional auction house with competent experts where I brought it only valued the painting at $5,000 to $7,000. The painting selling for $266,000 was astonishing to everyone involved and its purchase price set a world record for this artist.

MORAL: With the right professional, it is a good idea to trust the auction and consignment process. The auction process for certain things has a way of revealing value that no one, not even the so-called experts, thought was possible.

 3   MICHAEL PRICE DRESS KNIFE, $93,000

This extraordinary one-of-a-kind knife was made by a knife maker in San Francisco, California, in the late 1800s. This knife, as beautiful as it looks, would not be easy to research in order to find out how much it's worth. It's not signed Michael Price; instead it is signed, "M. Price San Francisco." It is a rare artifact from the Gold Rush days of San Francisco's past.

In the old days of San Francisco, flush with the spoils of metal taken from nearby golden hills, many a fine citizen pranced or strutted through banquets or other social extravaganzas wearing dress daggers and the like, imitating pashas and knights of the past. The richest of those partygoers might have had a knife like this. In the 1870s or 1880s when this dagger was first made, it likely cost $200 or $300, which was a small fortune.

Given its value and that it was obviously a miracle of highbrow knife craft,

It is only by searching for treasures that one is found. M. Price dress dagger found among debris and sold via Greg Martin Auctions. *Greg Martin Auctions*

you would think that such a spectacular knife would have been handed down protectively throughout its history as a precious object. Something to be guarded, cherished, and taken care of, but that was not the case. I wish I knew what grand old dude it was made for, what hip it found itself clanking against, and which ribbon cutting or giving a key to the city soiree it found its way to. But of the journey this dagger took from the deep recesses of the Barbary Coast heyday of San Francisco's past, I know nothing. I only know where I found it.

At some point, the last person who owned this knife got the idea to wrap it in a dirty blue silk cloth and then put this package of preciousness into a greasy zip lock bag. I found it stashed behind the door of a small derelict sofa side table that was stacked with other forgotten furniture high in an attic of a rundown and debris-filled home. I have no idea how long it hid there. I brought it to Greg Martin of Greg Martin Auctions, who played me like an *Antiques Roadshow* sucker fish before hooking me with the revelation that this dagger was worth between $45,000 to $50,000. I consigned the dagger to his company and it sold at auction for $93,000.

MORAL: Don't assume that a roomful of junk only contains junk. Treasure could be hidden amongst the debris of someone's carelessness. Don't want to get your hands dirty? Then hire a professional to go through everything. Just make sure that one way or another everything in a home is gone through.

4 TIFFANY GRANDFATHER CLOCK SOLD AT CLARS FOR $4,500

There was a wealthy family who lived in Southern California. On one side of the family were the founders of a major department store, a place that catered

What has your family forgotten about in storage? This Tiffany grandfather's clock stored for many years sold for $4,500. *Fine Estate Liquidation*

to those with more dough than your average Sears and Roebuck shopper. They were style and taste makers for their little part of the world. On the other side of the family was a patriarch, who had established one of the many oil companies that emerged out of the rich California landscape. The marriage that brought these two families together must have set the Los Angeles community of the early 1920s abuzz. They lived, they prospered, they passed.

Their personal property was bequeathed to family members, who moved away from the sunny homes they once owned. At least one of them moved to the San Francisco area, which is where I met the great-great-granddaughter of this family, at the open shipping bay of a large moving and storage facility.

Her family's stuff had been divided many times over the years. Each time they divided it, the family would meet at this storage facility and pick out various items for their own homes or the homes of their children. The day I got there was the end of the road for this process. Everyone had all that they wanted or needed now. Styles change from one generation to the next and one's valuable antique is another's unbearable dust-collecting object. It was time for them to sell what remained after this final cull of their family's possessions.

I was there to make an offer on the items that had been stored, but had a different idea about whether or not I should make an offer after I saw the breadth of what they had. I knew that it would be so much better for this family if they allowed me to act as an agent of sale for their stuff and they agreed.

A little side note about items marked Tiffany and Co.: Not all of them were actually made by Tiffany. Tiffany also had a large retail store and brought in many fabulous items from different parts of the world, put their name on them, and then sold those items in their store. Such was the case with this grandfather's clock, which, after being placed in a large regional auction house, sold for $4,500.

MORAL: Take care with inherited family property that has found its way, for whatever reason, into storage. Also, just because it is marked Tiffany and Co. doesn't mean it was actually made by them.

5 LANDOLPHI VIOLIN—CARLO FERNANDO LANDOLPHI MILAN, CIRCA 1755, SOLD FOR $59,750 AT CHRISTIE'S

I got a call from a conservator, who had an interesting client. Sometime in her client's past, she had been a first violinist for a major symphony orchestra. Unfortunately for her, early in her career while walking with a friend, she stepped off a curb and was hit by a speeding motorist. After spending a long time in the hospital, it was discovered that her long-term memory was gone. Her concert days were over and her family, doing the best they could, cared for her for many years in her own home. At some point, a conservator was appointed by the courts to see to her needs.

Taking care of her was costly, so the conservator needed to figure out what parts of the assets that she had left might be used to see to her care for the coming years. It was known that the violin that she used to play in the symphony had some value, although no one knew who made it or exactly how much it was worth.

The violin had been stored for many years in a bank vault in Oakland, California. I met with a supervisor there and was given the violin, so that I could find out who made it and what its potential value might be.

This was in 2002, before anyone had much access to the Internet, and the only way to figure things out was to first make a lot of phone calls. Many so-called experts told me that the violin couldn't possibly be authentic, but through perseverance, I finally located a violin maker, who not only sold stringed instruments to the symphony, but serviced them as well. There is no way that anyone can determine where an item might be sold until it has first been ascertained precisely what the item is, if it's authentic, what is its condition, and so on.

Roland Feller, the expert I brought the violin to, authenticated that it was made by Carlo Fernando Landolphi, an important Italian violin maker. Even

To learn who made a violin, peep into the "F" hole. This is one made by Landolphi and sold via Christie's. *Christie's*

given its poor condition, when it went up for auction at Christie's, it hammered for an impressive $53,000.

MORAL: Always check with more than one expert for their feedback about what your items is, and what its potential value might be. The three questions you need to get answers to: What is the item? What is its condition? Which sales channel has delivered the best sales results for an item like mine?

6 · GEORGIAN-STYLE GILT BRONZE MOUNTED BRACKET CLOCK; SOLD AT CLARS AUCTION FOR $50,000

Let's say that you have inherited the personal property of someone who lived in a distant city and you didn't really know them well or what their collecting habits might have been. So, because you didn't really know them and because you have many of your own pressing matters to attend to, you think that you will book a flight, arrive at that person's home, make a series of quick decisions about the disposal of their personal property, and in a few days get back to your happy home, pleased to be done with the whole process in such a short and efficient timespan. I see this on at least a monthly basis: people too busy to protect the value of their estates.

Massive 4-foot tall English bracket clock. *Fine Estate Liquidation*

What you might've missed is the fact that this person had a storage unit full of various items that you had no idea about because no one ever told you, and you weren't careful enough when going through the decedent's personal papers to notice that they have been paying monthly storage bills for years. This is what makes episodes of *Storage Wars* so compelling to watch. I don't know with any certainty, but it is an easy speculation that a certain percentage of all the storage lockers that have been seized and sold at auction come from estates where someone passed away and no one knew there was a storage locker anywhere, never mind what might be in it.

The English Bracket clock that you see here came out of a storage locker filled with many other vintage and antique clocks. In this particular case, it was part of an estate where the contents of the storage locker were known

Antiques from China are rising in value at a tremendous rate, so look for porcelains and textiles. Sold via Clars, Oakland, California. *Fine Estate Liquidation*

about, but it could easily have been the case that the family of the man who owned them might never have been informed about them. Use caution: take your time going through the personal papers when you look through an estate.

This clock, even though it was missing its pendulum, sold for a mighty $50,000.

MORAL: Sometimes all the best stuff, the legendary treasures that get found in an estate, are in storage. Make it your business as an executor or a family member to discover whether or not any of an estate's personal property is located outside of the home, in storage, or more likely in a safety deposit box.

7 CHINESE BLANC DE CHINE PORCELAIN FIGURAL GROUP, FEATURING THE TWIN IMMORTALS, SOLD AT CLARS FOR $35,000

There was a man who lived in an upscale neighborhood in Monterey, California, who passed away. His children, because they had so many disagreements amongst them, could only make one decision about his stuff with any degree of unanimity and that was to pack the whole lot of their father's possessions up into large wooden crates and bring them to a storage facility in Castroville, California.

After a few years of paying for storage, his daughter called me and asked if I would be willing to help her appraise, photograph, and inventory the contents of those storage crates so that all of her siblings would be able to pick and choose the items that they wanted to retain. Each family member would then have the value of the item they picked deducted from their portion of their father's estate.

My wife Valletta and I traveled to the storage facility and began the laborious process of unpacking the storage crates onto tables, matching everything up, and photographing it all.

In the process, we found this Chinese Blanc de Chine porcelain figural group. We did not know how much this item was worth when we first saw it, which is not surprising. Asian antiquities are rising in value almost on a daily basis, so much so that an item that was worth $1,000 yesterday may be worth $10,000 tomorrow. Asian porcelains are among the most sought after antiques in the marketplace today.

Family members chose what they wanted and were held back from taking everything because now that values had been appended to the contents of their father's estate, no one wanted to take too much and have it count against their portions of the estate. This process acted like a brake to the forward motion of those in the family who wanted too much.

Now what to do with the rest of it? Castroville is in Monterey Bay County, far from the bright city lights and is not a hot auction kind of town. In fact, the auction houses that are in the area, as nice as they were, were not really that large, nor did they have the worldwide reach needed to generate extremely high auction results.

Our client relied on our acumen and experience and followed our recommendations, which was to remove the best items from her father's storage and have them sold in an auction house that had an international audience of buyers. It was only because of the high profile of the auction house that we chose that this family was able to enjoy the results of the sale of this Blanc de Chine figural group, which sold for an astounding and surprising $35,000.

MORAL: Remember, without an appraisal, you as an executor really do not know how to evenly divide a decedent's personal property. Also, ask the professional you are working with if the property that they are suggesting should go to auction is really going to an auction house that is appropriate for the property being consigned.

8 COCA COLA COLLECTION SOLD AT DAN MORPHYS FOR $34,175

I walked up a pebbled path through a kind of Japanese garden and knocked on the door of a house near California State-Berkeley. I was there on a referral from an attorney I had previously done work for to meet two sisters whose father had passed away. The house was nice, but no palace and nothing about its outside appearance would suggest what might be on the inside.

Although reproductions of these abound in the marketplace, when genuine, the best of these can sell for over $10,000. *Fine Estate Liquidation*

What is it? How much is it worth? Where do you sell it? Answering these three questions is important. We sold this Coca Cola collection via Dan Morphy's. *Fine Estate Liquidation*

The father had no strange secrets, but he did have several collecting passions. The first one I saw was his glass insulator collection, about 200 of them all lined up in rows within lit glass cabinets. He was a member of several glass insulator collecting associations. Those were interesting and no doubt had value, but what stopped me in my tracks was what I saw hanging like many colored ovals and disks all over the kitchen walls. There before me, where they had hung for years and years, was a fairly extensive collection of Coca Cola tip trays, originally made in the early 1900s. And in the den, there was a large framed Coca Cola festoon, which you can see a detail of in the picture shown.

My wife Valetta and I photographed this collection, researched them all, sent a few images to Dan Morphy's Auctions, and determined from the feedback that these tip trays were indeed authentic. We packed up the lot and sent them to Morphy's, where they sold collectively for $34,175. A good result, considering their condition.

MORAL: Remember that value determines venue and venue determines value. These clients, because they allowed us to handle their father's estate, using multiple marketing and sales paths, were able to enjoy an overall greater income for the items.

9 1967 MORGAN SOLD AT AN ESTATE SALE IN SONOMA FOR $18,000

In Sonoma, a place that sees several million wine-tasting tourists on a yearly basis, was a corner house on a tree-lined street. The house had a split-rail fence holding onto the edge of a well-kept lawn. I could see old cast iron garden furniture rusting on the wide porch, as I walked up the steps to knock on the door.

The son of the decedent opened the door and showed me around his father's home. This might sound strange, but the house was almost too clean. It was like all the little things that can make an estate sale successful, as well as the bigger, more valuable items also necessary to attracting shoppers, had, for whatever reason, been removed. What was there was still nice, though, so I was at least interested in doing a sale for this family. While discussing sale details with this man, it came out that there were also items in storage and he wanted to know if it would be okay to sell them as well. Without knowing what was in storage, I said that would be fine.

When I and my staff arrived back at the home to set up the sale, there in the garage was a 1967 Morgan. Oh my, that was a surprise. Apparently it had been up on blocks in storage for years. It didn't run, but its interior and exterior was in beautiful original condition.

For our sales, we do extensive marketing and send out over 3,700 emails to

This Morgan is one of my favorite items we have ever sold. It's important to note that you can sell high-value items at an estate sale. *Fine Estate Liquidation*

announce each one, and we posted notices on Craigslist, as well as put ads in several local newspapers, so imagine our surprise when the man who came to buy the car had not seen any of these notices. What he did see, while driving through his neighborhood on the Friday morning of the sale, was one of our estate signs hanging on a tree and decided to pull over and see what was for sale. He hadn't planned on spending $18,000 that morning for a car, but that's what he did. He went home, got his wife, hitched up a trailer to his truck, came back, and then we all pushed the Morgan up the trailer ramp and he drove away a happy man.

MORAL: If you have items in storage that are connected to the estate, let your liquidator know and ask if they can incorporate the stored items with the estate sale. Always make sure that all avenues of marketing are employed to get shoppers to a sale. Sometimes it's the Internet marketing that gets the shoppers, and sometimes it's one of those well placed estate sales signs that they have hung from a tree.

10 PAIR OF LOUIS XVI-STYLE MARBLE TOP COMMODES, CIRCA 1900, SOLD AT CLARS AUCTION FOR $16,000

Not one of us knows everything. Even we, who are recognized as professionals or experts in the antiques and collectibles field, can be baffled. What separates a pro from an amateur is that our guesses are better. We have spent years and years noticing the way small details can elevate value, or the fact that what makes something so special that a buyer ponies up a wad of cash for an item often hinges on the way a shade of patina is mellow enough to glow or is too dull to notice. But we don't know everything.

For instance, take these Louis XVI-style commodes. None of us thought they were extraordinary; nice, yes, but remarkable? No. I knew they were not period pieces and had been made in a later period, but I liked them enough to believe they should be in an auction, rather than one of our estate sales. Good thing I did.

The people at the auction house pretty much confirmed my opinion and wrote their description reflecting what we all thought about them. The day of

Positive surprises! No one knows it all, but experts generally make better guesses. Sold via Clars Auctions. *Fine Estate Liquidation*

Sometimes furniture is composed of both antique and recent components. This is known as a piece that has been "married with older parts." *Fine Estate Liquidation*

the auction came and they hammered down for $16,000, a result that surprised everyone.

MORAL: Sometimes it pays to take a risk with the auction process. There are many worldwide buyers who often have greater expertise in certain fields, and when you have two or more of them bidding against each other for an item, the results can be dramatic. It turns out that what made this pair of dressers so valuable was not the dressers themselves, but the hardware. The hardware was from a much earlier period and someone wanted it.

11 THREE SPANISH GUITARS (SANTO HERNADEZ GUITAR PICTURED) SOLD AT CHRISTIES FOR $14,000

In a silent basement apartment lived a solitary man without much, if any, connection to his family. He lived on the edge, one or two rungs above the poverty line. His apartment was jammed with stuff. He had hand built many little shelving units and nailed those onto the walls between the many pictures and paintings he had already hung there. The effect was of an apartment with walls that were not walls, but more like wind-shifting tapestries interrupted here and there by these little homemade shelves holding the many shiny gewgaws of his fascination.

He loved minerals and mineral specimens and at some point in his past, he took up

Fine Estate Liquidation

Even items with damage, if they are rare and wonderful, have value.
We sold this pair of Meissen figurines via eBay. *Fine Estate Liquidation*

lapidary and gem faceting and had all of the equipment for this hobby packed helter skelter into his small apartment. His space was like a mini episode of the TV show *Hoarders*. There was hardly a free space to turn around in. I got called to give a bid on the contents of his place after he passed away. I want to say that the person asking me to make the buyout bid was a caring professional who had been around the block more than a few times when it came to situations like this … they were professional alright, but not the caring kind.

I had given him bids in the past for other estates and on each occasion that I had been asked to make one, I always said the same thing, "You know, if you allowed me to sell the contents of this place on behalf of the estate, that the heirs will get more money don't you?" And his response was always the same, "We don't have time for that. We have to clear out this place. The rent and other expenses are mounting and we have to move on."

I bid for the contents of this apartment against three other estate liquidators, and my bid was roughly twice as high as the next highest. So, I bought it. In the closet, stacked against the wall, under piles of clothes, were three guitar cases and when I opened them up, I saw that the guitars in them were old-style Flamenco guitars. I sent them to auction and they sold collectively for $14,000.

MORAL: Always, always, always hire a professional to act as an agent of sale for the personal property of an estate. Get someone to work for, and protect, the interest of the estate.

12 PAIR OF MEISSEN FIGURAL GROUPS SOLD FOR $12,280 ON EBAY

The Meissen facts of life: First, if it says Meissen, it probably isn't Meissen. Second, not all crossed sword marks are Meissen.

I remember seeing porcelains in my grandmother's house. Courtly ladies embraced by frill-cuffed fancy jacketed men … a few of them seemed to have been captured in the mid-step of a waltz that had taken place over a century ago. But these were knockoffs made in Japan or Hong Kong post WWII. We didn't have the dough to be out collecting fine porcelains.

But your grandparents might have. I have even heard of some of these extraordinary Meissen porcelains coming back from Germany as part of what was collected, or maybe it's better described as appropriated from a bombed-out home, by a U.S. serviceman. This happened more than you might think. A few days ago as of this writing, a woman called to ask what I thought about the value of an entire china dinner service that her father had brought back home. She was a little embarrassed to talk about it, but these things happened.

You could look on the bottom of 10,000 porcelain figures for the crossed swords mark of Meissen porcelains or the shield mark of true Royal Vienna and you will not find those marks, but that shouldn't stop you from looking. By all means look … who knows what you will find? And if you find the right mark under your piece, you can expect to cash in and receive what might seem like a lot of money for them.

The picture you see on P. 186 of the Meissen figural group was one of two that came out of a San Francisco home, and although each figure had damage, like a few fingers missing, we sold them on eBay for $12,280.

MORAL: It's all in the marks. The figures pictured, without the crossed swords marks underneath them, would have sold for many thousands of dollars less. Also, to get a great sales result on eBay, you have to have a well-established feedback rating. If you do not have a well-established eBay profile, bidders will not bid as high of a price for your items as they might for sellers with much greater reputations. eBay buyers can be skittish. Your solution is to find a professional who already has a well-established eBay store to act on your behalf.

13 JOHN COBURN AUSTRALIAN PAINTING, $10,648

Once upon a time, there was a husband and wife who lived on the Gold Coast of Australia. They owned and operated a pawn shop there for many years, buying or loaning money for whatever sort of fancy trinket their customers brought in—likely heaps and piles of fancy black opals and diamond-bedecked cocktails rings.

When they retired, they moved to California to live out their golden years. When the husband passed away, the stuff they had collected became something of a burden for the wife to manage. She hired an organizer to help her lighten her load and they called me. She was a little white-haired woman about eighty years old. She was a doll and utterly fantastic, with a spectacular smile; oh, and she liked to wear black leather pants. She was a gem and one of the happier people I have met. In this business, so many people who call me, because they are facing such mind-numbing challenges, are not very happy. But she was. She still had a life to lead, and by gosh, that is what she was going to do—live.

She had many fun things to look at and the organizer helping her was astute and definitely looking out for the woman's best interest. I suggested that they consign her personal property to one of my upcoming estate sales, which is what she did.

In the mix amongst some of the paintings that she consigned to us was an odd one. It was very colorful and abstract and demanded my attention. I did some research on the artist and discovered that he was important back in her homeland, so I sent the painting to Bonhams in Australia, where it sold for

You might think this is a painting that your 10-year-old could paint, but that's not the point. Collectors see it differently. Sold via Bonhams in Australia. *Fine Estate Liquidation*

$10,648, which was a much higher price than any amount I would have been able to receive for her painting here in the States.

MORAL: Again, value determines venue. In order to generate the highest income for an item, you have to make sure that the item in question is being offered in the right sales venue. America was not the place to sell an Aboriginal painting from Australia. By sending it back to where it had first been created, its esthetic could be more appreciated, and the buyers for this category of art could then be reached in a more impactful manner.

It's all about the packaging. If these Hot Wheels were out of their packs, their value would have plummeted. *Fine Estate Liquidation*

14 REDLINE HOT WHEELS SOLD AT AN ESTATE SALE FOR $8,500

When going through a house, especially when it is nice, of course I get excited when I see jewelry, whatever silver there is, the china, and any of the many other items that have some value. Estate sales are costly to stage and conduct, so there has to be enough items of value plainly in sight for me to be able to make the determination that I can help a family with their estate.

But it is when I am led into a garage, basement, or an attic, and it is stuffed with boxes and boxes, with sheets or slip covers covering up a bunch of old stuff … that's when the antiques antenna goes up like an old car aerial and I begin tuning in and wonder what's in there. What has been stashed away and forgotten about? Is there any treasure? It is in places like these that I most anticipate finding a marvel, a gem, or a piece of history, and can't wait to get a chance to sift through it all.

We were setting up an estate like that. The house was filled with nice things and was mostly orderly in the main part of the house, but it did have the fabled stacks of boxes in the garage. The man who owned the house once ran a service station in town with what I can only assume must have been a small store attached to it.

Back in the late 1960s to early 1970s, one of the items he sold was Hot Wheels. But he didn't sell all of them because somehow a large box of them were brought back to his garage and stacked there, along with many other boxes. A member of our staff found the box of cars, worth so much more now that forty years had passed.

There were about a hundred of them, and I personally researched each and every one, checking to see if there were any rare variants, and after my research, I placed a price of $8,500 on them. The guy who bought the Hot Wheels handed me a check for them sight unseen as he walked in the door of the sale. He was the first person in line, and had been there since the wee hours of the morning.

MORAL: Don't assume that you can't get big bucks for high value collectibles at an estate sale because you can, if you know what you are doing. And yes, it is also true that if you had wanted to spend about sixty to seventy hours of your time to list and sell them on eBay, you could have earned more for your estate. Time will add value, but how much time you add to the process is dependent on how much time you have. There are only so many hours in a day.

15 ALAN ADLER MODERN GEORGIAN STERLING FLATWARE; SOLD VIA OUR WEBSITE FOR $8,150

More now than even in the days of the famed Hunt Brothers' manipulation of the silver markets, the silver market is hot. Very hot! The price of silver in the last few years has gone from $15 an ounce to a high of close to $50 an ounce. This created frenzy in the silver markets and set up a collision between utility value and financial value. Also, this escalation in value happened at the same time as two other important concurrent factors. Millions of Americans found themselves needing money because of their own economic woes at the same time that many people began asking themselves, "How relevant is this silver to my life, anyway?" Silver is formal. We don't use it anymore to impress our friends, neighbors, or other family members with our wealth or sophistication. We dine much more casually now, and who wants to polish it, anyway? Most of us don't.

Because of this lack of relevance, and because so many people needed the money just at the time that silver was climbing through the roof of believ-ability, people began seeking buyers for their silver heirlooms. The market-place was more than ready for them and thousands of new shops opened up across America to buy silver. These dealers were only concerned about one thing and one thing only, though: to buy as much silver on one day and sell it the next. The place that these metals dealers sell the silver that you sell them is to refineries. Refiners don't care a hoot about an heirloom. They need to process a river of metal every day, so they melt it. Most of the family silver sold to dealers in the last few years has been melted and now exists as an ingot or bar only.

I happen to love silver, both for how it can be used to express creative visions in jewelry, as well as how it can be made into objects of beauty that also have a functional utility. I make a practice to go through the buckets of silver that the metals buyers have stored it in until they have enough of it to bring a load down to the refiners.

I find stuff in those buckets; little miracle treasures. Sometimes I find more than little stuff, though. Sometimes I find monumental silver, like this set of Alan Adler Silver in the Modern Georgian pattern. Alan Adler is one of the best, most sought after contemporary silversmiths in America. I bought this set from a metals guy, who was going to melt it. I not only saved it from the swallowing fires of the smelters crucible, I made a hefty profit as well. I sold it on eBay for $8,150.

Thinking of selling your silver pattern for melt value? First look it up. Some flatware patterns are worth many times their metal value. Sold via eBay. *Fine Estate Liquidation*

it on eBay for $8,150.

But the thing that bugs me is how the person who first sold it to the metals guy did not know, or even how to know, that this set had way more value as a collectible than a melted puddle of metal. I wonder what executor or heir made this mistake.

MORAL: Never ever sell an item without first knowing what the item is. Don't know? Don't sell. Don't know how to figure it all out? Get help.

16 ALICE CHITTENDEN PAINTING SOLD AT AN ESTATE SALE FOR $7,100

There was a good nephew in his late fifties or early sixties. His aunt and uncle had been in the antiques business for many years and were even a bit famous for their store on Market Street in the 1970s or 1980s. They hung out with the Butterfield and Butterfield big-wigs, John Gallo and Bernard Osher, who were afoot and hammering down auction bids like sailors slamming down tankards on old wooden bars. His aunt and uncle were part of the glory days of the antiques trade in San Francisco I hear about every once in awhile. This nephew helped them while they had their store, and continued to help his aunt long after what I assume was her separation from her husband, and into the advancement of her old age and eventual passing.

It takes having access to the right database to value a decorative painting like this, or you may sell it for way too little. Sold via an estate sale.
Fine Estate Liquidation

When his aunt had to go into assisted living, the only thing anyone could think to do with her stuff was to put it into storage. I met the nephew in front of a roll-up door of a storage locker. When he opened it, I could take a step or two into it, but I couldn't see everything, and neither one of us had any real idea what might be in there. She had two storage lockers jumble piled with stuff.

I liked what of it that I could see, and suggested that he consign the two storage lockers to my company and we would fold their contents into one of our upcoming estate sales. He thought that was a good idea, so that's what we did.

The prized piece in the storage locker was a floral still life painting by Alice Chittenden we sold for $7,100 right off the wall of the estate sale we presented it at.

MORAL: A result like this by an estate liquidator only comes about after they have made a careful analysis of the marketplace, so that they have learned not just what the value of the painting is, but also whether or not an estate sale or an auction is the best sales venue to sell the painting.

17 AMEDEE JOULLIN PAINTING SOLD AT AN ESTATE SALE FOR $7,100

A call from a man who was referred to us by a realtor had me arriving to a house located on the downslope of one of San Francisco's many hills. I was met at the door by a handsome man who was one of two brothers.

Their mom used to work at one of the most exclusive private clubs in San Francisco, the Pacific Union Club. I am sure she heard just above the clink of whiskey glasses the deals that were being made. She worked there for years and at the end of her time, she was given a painting by the membership. She hung the painting in the living room of her home for years, and it really was the fanciest thing she owned.

The family lived a modest, quiet life in that home, and I am guessing because of how the painting was presented to me, they thought it was nice, but not particularly valuable. But it did have value. It could even have had major value, except that it had a multitude of condition issues: a cracked surface, old repairs, and a bit of water damage. A lot of people might have thought that it was a painting past its prime, or one whose value was too diminished by its condition to be worth much, but I liked it. I did some research and after finding out that the artist was listed, I set the price at $7,100, even with its condition issues. The person who bought it eventually donated it to the Crocker Art Museum in Sacramento, where they embarked on the expensive process of restoring it.

MORAL: As in real estate, where it is location, location, location that determines value, in the world of antiques and collectibles, it's condition, condition, condition. But that does not mean that just because your object has condition issues that it does not have value. Paintings, especially by listed artists, are more often than not well worth the cost of their repair.

18   TWO MOORCROFT INKWELLS SOLD FOR $5,200 AT RAGO AUCTIONS

A couple of years ago, I did a buyout of a first-floor flat full of stuff that I folded into the sale I conducted for another estate. The stuff I bought was just stuff and none of it was worth a great deal, except there were two ceramic inkwells I found in a box that had been stashed in the basement of the building and forgotten. As I mentioned, even estate liquidators don't know everything, and when I don't know what something is, I tend to put it away until I can figure it out. I knew that these two inkwells were nice and were made by Moorcroft Pottery, but because they were rare, I really couldn't figure out how much they were worth.

A few years later while going through some old auction catalogs, I saw one of the inkwells that sold for over $1,000. I contacted the auctioneer and it turned out that one of the two design patterns for the inkwell was called Eventide, which was a much sought after design. The auctioneer was David Rago and I was told he was excited about these two inkwells. I sent them to Ragos and they sold separately in two lots for a total of $5,200. I think the results for the Eventide inkwell even set a record for the results it achieved.

MORAL: Haste makes waste. Jumping to act before the starting gun will

Even paintings with condition issues can have a high value. This Amedee Joullin painting is a good example and it was sold by us at an estate sale. *Fine Estate Liquidation*

Take your time. There is no great rush to take everything to market, especially if you don't know what it is. These inkwells were sold via Rago Auctions. *Rago Auctions*

leave you with less income. Take time. In the world of antiques and collectibles, time adds value.

🏷 19 GROUP OF ROCK 'N' ROLL POSTERS PRIVATELY SOLD FOR $75,000

Here is a hard story to tell. A number of years ago, I got a call from a semi-professional organizer. She helped realtors and attorneys organize and dispose of the personal property of the estates that they represented. She had one of their houses that she wanted me to look at to make a buyout offer of its personal property.

I, and two other estate liquidators on separate occasions, sorted through the personal property of this home and then each of us came up with our buyout prices. On several occasions before making an offer, and even once after giving her my offer, I suggested to this organizer that she seriously con-

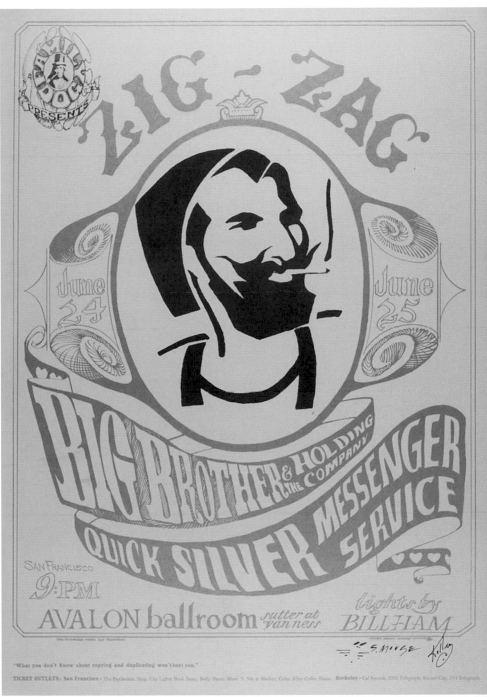

Estate buyouts may seem like your best way out, but ask yourself if you really know what you're selling. We sold these posters to a group of private collectors.

sider an on-site estate sale as an alternative to a buyout. I told her the estate would be better off with two thirds of the income from a sale of the estate's personal property, rather than it would from the income they would receive from a buyout, which is essentially the wholesale purchase of a house's entire contents for one fixed price. She declined each time I suggested this.

It was a nice house, but nothing extraordinary. Filled with years of living and accumulations, nothing seemed particularly valuable. My offer was the highest one that she received, so I was awarded the right to buy the estate's personal property.

Downstairs in the basement, lying flat and literally sandwiched between layers of building materials, was something wrapped in a large black plastic garbage bag. When we dislodged it and opened up the bag, we discovered what can only be described as the Holy Grail of rock 'n' roll posters from San Francisco's Fillmore West, and The Family Dog. These were two of the most famous rock clubs in the country in the 1960s. There were 73 posters, and most of them were in almost mint condition.

MORAL: A buyout may seem like the most expeditious way to, in a sense, get rid of all of your problems, but it is not necessarily the best way to generate the highest income for your estate. A group of posters like this, or any other specialty items that might be found, need to

Look for gold quartz items, as many of them are valuable and if they are old and grand enough, they can sell for many thousands of dollars.
Sold via Michaans Auctions. *Fine Estate Liquidation*

be handled carefully, and much work needs to be done before a sales result like the one we achieved can be accomplished.

20 GOLD QUARTZ PRESENTATION CANE SOLD FOR $3,500 AT MICHAANS AUCTIONS, ALAMEDA

Just after gold was discovered at Sutter's Mill in 1849, San Francisco, already a well-established city, began to experience a great influx of people from all over the world. One of them was a German immigrant who came here after first trying his hand at various enterprises in Philadelphia. He was one of the few miners successful in the gold fields, making an astonishing $5,000 in a short time period. That was a ton of money in those days. After losing his fortune due to sickness, he became the sole sales agent for the Tilton McFarlane Safe Company, which established his wealth and prestige.

He built a big house on the top of Broadway Street in the late 1800s, and just before the Great Earthquake of 1906, he had the Victorian he had built moved down from its perch on the hill to Van Ness Avenue, which at the time was like a grand boulevard of incredible homes. This large house stayed in the same family for well over 100 years and it was one of his descendants who contacted me to assist him in selling his family's personal property. Everything in the house was original and period, except that the kitchen and one of the bathrooms had been remodeled.

I know you may be asking why I'm telling you about this house, which obviously was a mansion and not a modest home that something extraordinary was found in.

The reason I am telling you about the object that came from this house is because I made a miscalculation about it. I knew what it was and was so certain about its value, that I declined an offer of $5,000 for it. Instead, I decided to take my chances by allowing it to be sold at an auction. It turned out that I was wrong. Instead of the $5,000 I could have sold this gold quartz presentation cane for at one of our estate sales, I watched, with humorous horror, as it sold for $3,500 in an auction. Still not a bad result, but I wish I had taken the earlier offer. No one gets it right each and every time.

MORAL: You are not always going to get it right. Some valuable things will sell for less than your perception of what you think they are worth. It is the aggregated results of all sales that you need to track. At auction or an estate sale, there are always items that exceed your expectation, meet them, or fall below them. It is the nature of the enterprise.

Chapter 10

WHEN SHOULD YOU BE CRAZY ENOUGH TO CONDUCT YOUR OWN ESTATE SALE?

THE SHORT ANSWER TO THIS QUESTION IS: ALMOST NEVER!

Considering the many pitfalls that a professional has to overcome while conducting an estate sale, you would be wise as a complete novice not to undertake doing your own. In fact, the most sensible thing you could do is to run away as fast as you can from the idea of doing your own estate sale. Even just the idea is something you want to approach cautiously and never casually entertain. At the end of the actual task of doing your own estate sale, the sweat, effort, and exertion of it all, may not seem to have been entirely worth it.

I will suggest many times in this chapter that you seek the assistance of professionals, who have many more years of experience dealing with the complications that arise from having to set up and sell personal property from a home than you do. If you proceed on your own, it may seem like there is no end to the emotional upheavals you'll have to face or the tactical roadblocks that you will have to overcome. You could get robbed or have your house burglarized. Because of your lack of experience, you could get so thoroughly picked by a professional picker, you will sell for a pittance your estate's most valuable items. You could get so overwhelmed by an estate sale's setup that it takes you months to get through it, which could complicate or stall the sale of the real estate.

In short, there are thousands of things that can and will go wrong. Minor complications can turn into big headaches. The public will seem overly bold, brazen, and incredibly rude. They will push every single one of your emotional hot buttons. Estate sales shoppers do not care in the same way that you care about your family's personal property. I'm not saying all of them are like this, but the few who are will leave you feeling traumatized.

Estate sales are wild and crazy events that have kinetic lives all their own. They are like roller coaster rides set on high intensity. As a professional, I think at best I am only ever able to manage and shape the chaos of a sale, not control it. If you have any issue at all with needing to control everything, or if you are the shy and retiring type, then the mad-house antics of glassy-eyed shoppers and the chaotic atmosphere that shimmers the air of your typical estate sale may be too much for you to handle.

You may think that you have approached the idea of doing your own estate sale as any good driver might an intersection, expecting other drivers to play nice and observe basic traffic rules; red light means stop and green light means go. The estate sales shopping public is all about that green light, though, and are on the go, go, go, especially that part of the herd that is pushy and rude. To them, because they can smell how inexperienced you are, you will resemble a lamb that has been led to your slaughter.

Dealers and pickers, as well as collectors, make a ton of money purchasing goods directly from families staging the kind of sale you're contemplating: a private, nonprofessional estate sale. As a novice, you cannot be as prepared and won't have the knowledge or expertise that professionals do to properly value your estate's personal property. This is no small shortcoming; if you do your own estate sale, you will be giving away money and maybe lots of it.

Advertising a privately run estate sale is an invitation that publicly announces to thousands of people in your town or city that you, an amateur, are opening up the once private sanctuary of your mom or dad to sell all of their possessions on a first-come, first-served basis.

· ·

Remember that if you are seriously considering conducting your own estate sale, you will have to prepare yourself emotionally ...

· ·

The public will be unpredictable and often disrespectful. You can count on it. They will bring their argumentative and free-for-all shopping styles. They will "act out" and verbally fight with each other. They will jostle, grab, and shout. After the first rush of them has come and gone, you will stand in stunned amazement, mouth agape, wondering how in the world you managed to survive their onslaught. Can people really be so rude? You bet they can! You will encounter behavior in your loved one's home the likes of which you haven't seen since that disastrous, argumentative Thanksgiving dinner that happened long ago.

These shoppers, especially the first 60 or 70 of them, might in fact care about the humanity of your home and may even be otherwise respectful given a different situation, but as a group shopping at your estate sale, they will seem insensitive, abrupt, or extraordinarily rude.

Remember that if you are seriously considering conducting your own estate sale, you will have to prepare yourself emotionally, if you are to have any chance at dealing with the above. It is not impossible to conduct your own estate sale, but the road will be difficult and fraught with peril.

Organization is the key to a successful sale. Display your household items in a neat and tidy fashion. This will allow buyers to make quick decisions.

PRICING: WHERE THE DEVIL MEETS THE DETAILS

No matter how you determine what to price an item, and I don't care which price guides you use or if you searched the internet all day and night for the right values and priced each of them accordingly, you will be wrong. Now, I admit you will be much closer to understanding an item's value if you have done your homework, and you will certainly save yourself the anguish of selling a family heirloom for way too cheap, so researching is a good idea, but it's not the whole story. What I really want you to grasp is that even though researching is vitally important to having a successful sale, it is not the end all and be all of understanding how much you should charge for an item; experience is, and this is why estate liquidators get the big bucks.

PRICE STICKERS

If you do your own estate sale, and I don't care how tough you think you are or how firm your pre-estate sales resolve is about how much your personal property is worth, what you will quickly find out is that a price sticker is only a signal for a buyer to begin negotiations.

Get ready for what may seem like intense bickering, for big time deal making, for the back and forth of offer, and counteroffer. It's startling even to me how much of a life and death struggle some shoppers will make of this process. At the sale you are conducting, you will be meeting people who have been shopping at estate sales for years. They are consummate pros in the art of the haggle and do it every weekend. It's their job. They will often display aggressiveness in order to get you to lower your price. You'll get this each day of your sale and it will be unrelenting.

Also don't look for shoppers to take care of you. They won't let you know if your price was already ridiculously too low or if you should hold firm to the prices you have already set. You'll have to take care of yourself.

When you research the value for items down to their last detail and finally price them, sometimes the price that you're asking based upon your research is so high that it will stifle a sale rather than promote it. Pricing items too high is like throwing water on a fire. Estate sales shoppers must feel like they're getting a deal or they won't burn with the desire to purchase. I'm not saying you have to give the store away, but that it is important for you to create and sustain an atmosphere of excitement at your sales by pricing your items in amounts that shoppers can perceive as deals. Think about what department stores do to create buying frenzies. They have a sale.

For instance, you've discovered while researching a Fusse Movement wall clock that a similar one sold at a major auction for $5,000 and you naturally think your clock must be worth that much, so you price it for the same amount. What you don't know, and in fact don't know how to know, is if that clock listed as having sold at the auction for $5,000 really is the same kind of clock as the one you have.

Is the clock you have exactly the same, down to the clock case maker, clockworks and other criteria as the one that sold for so much money at the auction? Probably not. The possible outcome for this misattribution or overvaluation is that the public won't buy the clock. Or they will attempt to patiently explain to you that your prices are simply too high. And you, because you have a good and healthy dose of skepticism, won't really want to believe them. In either case, your sales efforts will suffer, and you'll still have the clock.

BUT ESTATE SALES PROFESSIONALS SAID 'NO' TO YOUR SALE

There are dozens of good reasons why you might consider conducting your own estate sale. The best one I've heard, the one that gets most people motivated to undertake the daunting job of staging and conducting their own estate sale, is: they simply couldn't get a professional estate liquidator to do it for them. It's a fact of the business that the job of staging a home and making it ready for an estate sale requires many staff hours and much management effort by an estate liquidator. If they do not perceive that there is enough of an aggregate value in the home to encourage them to take on your project, they will decline. It is for this reason that I have written this chapter.

TEN REASONS WHY PROS WON'T TOUCH YOUR ESTATE

1. Low financial value.
2. House is a huge mess.
3. House will be owner-occupied during the sale.
4. Bad neighborhood.
5. Client wants to micromanage the estate sale process.
6. Little or no street parking.
7. Family squabbles.
8. No proof that client has legal authority.
9. Too high of an expectation about values.
10. Client rejects estate liquidator's fees and commissions.

LOW FINANCIAL VALUE

The expenses for organizing and properly staging a house to make it ready for an estate sale can add up quickly. For us in the San Francisco Bay Area, where costs are high, even a small house with a modest amount of work in it will have expenses of between $2,000 and $3,000 to set up.

Estate sales shoppers must feel like they're getting a deal or they won't burn with the desire to purchase. It is important to create and sustain an atmosphere of excitement.

That's just the expense for staff time. So from an estate sale that generates $10,000, there wouldn't be much left over after paying our clients and staff expenses to compensate us for all of our efforts. For us, a $10,000 estate sale is too low a financial threshold for us to be able to help a client. But having said that, you should note that in many other parts of the country, estate liquidators with lower economies of scale are willing and able to accept projects with lower aggregate values. Check your phone book or the internet for local listings.

TRUE STORY: Recently I heard from a woman who was calling on behalf of her parents. She told me that the entire family had just flown into town in order to help her parents go through their grandparents' home. She wanted to know if I could come out to the family home on short notice and see the items that her parents wanted to sell because the family would be in town for only a few days. This happens all the time that family will arrive in from out of town, comb through and retain what they wish to keep from a family member's house, and then call an estate liquidator.

Problem: Estate value is too low to attract professional assistance.

Solution: If possible, consider less retention of valuables by family members.

But what happens in too many situations like this is that a family gathering becomes a free for all, whereby a family sorts through a house and retains only the best and most valuable items that it contains. They will do this and then brightly hope that someone can be found who will either stage an estate sale for them or who will take the rest of the contents off their hands via an estate buyout. This is a strategy that will almost never work.

To make a long story short, I wasn't able to help this particular family because they had taken too much of value from the house. Don't get me wrong. I totally believe that families must retain what is precious to the heart and I am even sure that this is sometimes what is also financially valuable. But where I think families hurt themselves is when they retain items only because of their financial value. It is the financial value of the personal property left over after a family goes through a house that will either attract an estate liquidator to take the project on or cause them to walk away.

HOUSE IS A HUGE MESS

Maybe you haven't seen your mom or dad or been in their house for a long time and didn't know of their hoarding tendencies, or maybe you did know that their house was tightly packed to the rafters with every kind of tin can, old newspaper, or bottle they could gather and stack skyward and have been dreading the day you would be the one to have deal with it. And then they unfortunately pass. I have walked into plenty of these homes. The ones that are the toughest to work in are those where food items have been improperly stored or where vermin have taken up residence. Houses like these will often need very different clean-out strategies than some estate liquidators can provide. The run-of-the-mill, stuffed-to-the-gills hoarder house, though, will definitely have much in them that can be sold. Don't assume that there are no buried treasures in them, either; it is in houses exactly like these that I have found some truly astounding treasures.

Problem: House is huge mess.

Solution 1: As much as possible, resist the temptation to call in a convoy of hauling trucks to cart it all away. Your mystification or genuine anger directed toward the hoarder in a situation like this will be of little or no help. Try and put your judgments aside and systematically start a sorting system to sift through the logjam of personal property that the house contains. Of course, during this process, you will want to throw things away; that's fine and you have this estate liquidator's permission to throw anything away that you absolutely know to be worth less than a half dollar. I know, that's going to be tough.

Solution 2: Call an estate liquidator or a professional organizer and be ready to pay them well to organize and make sense of the mass of objects in the home.

HOUSE WILL BE OWNER-OCCUPIED DURING SALE

This is a big time deal breaker for a lot of estate liquidators. Many of them simply will not agree to take on your project, if there are to be family members or other tenants in the home during their set up and conducting of your estate sale.

Also, it may prove to be a hardship for those who are occupying the house as well. An estate liquidator and their crew in your home is like an army of

A good rule of thumb for pricing furniture: If it is of recent vintage, price it at about 10 to 20 percent of its original cost.

strangers who have arrived and taken over. They will move everything around in order to set the place up for a sale and your home will quickly become less comfortable for anyone to live in.

Problem: House will be owner-occupied during sale.

Solution: Move out during the estate sales process. This is really the best way. If you need to keep items, then decide which of the rooms in your house can best be secured with a lock. This is where you can store the items you do not wish to sell.

HOUSE IS IN A BAD NEIGHBORHOOD

Staging an estate sale in a poor neighborhood needs to be separated and made distinct from the risk of staging an estate sale in a high crime rate neighborhood.

Personally, I have conducted estate sales in poor neighborhoods. That's no problem, as long as there is enough of value in the house to carry out a successful sale. But I won't, out of safety concerns for my clients, staff, and sales customers, conduct estate sales in high crime rate neighborhoods, if I think there is a probability of a crime or robbery occurring in or near the home.

TRUE STORY: About a year ago, I got a call from a woman whose uncle had recently passed away. He lived in a high crime rate neighborhood and his house was attracting the attention of some of the more unsavory neighbors who lived nearby and that on at least two separate occasions, attempts had been made to break into it. Her uncle also had a variety of guns.

This is usually enough information for me to decide that I just might be "too busy" to go out and see the situation, but I actually was too busy with an all-consuming hoarder house project and I didn't hear from her for over a month after that. It turns out that there were no other estate liquidators who wanted to help her. Other ones made and then broke appointments with her and in frustration, she finally called me back. It was during that conversation that she almost casually mentioned her uncle also had a large coin collection. You don't have to say "large coin collection" twice to perk me up and make me interested in a project, even if it is in a "bad neighborhood."

The upshot of the story is that we, on this client's behalf, were able to sell her uncle's entire coin collection for over $350,000. The way we were able to do this was to remove the valuable property away from the house in the bad neighborhood and sell it to a buyer willing to pay the highest purchase price.

CLIENT WANTS TO MICROMANAGE THE ESTATE SALE'S PROCESS

A client who insists on micromanaging an estate sale's process may find they are unable to attract the services of an estate liquidator. No one wants someone to be constantly looking over their shoulder. I know you are just trying to help and it is fine that you have information about items and insights about strategies that will enhance values. Everyone wants that. Being useful is great. But too often it is the case with a client who micromanages, who hovers over all the details, or questions every decision a professional makes, that they get perceived as someone whose efforts may hinder a sale's best possible outcome.

Estate liquidators will tend to distance themselves from a client like this as quickly as possible and not work with them.

A client who insists on micromanaging an estate sale's process may find they are unable to attract the services of an estate liquidator. No one wants someone to be constantly looking over their shoulder.

HOW CAN YOU KNOW IF YOU ARE THAT TYPE OF CLIENT? That's easy. If you can answer yes to any of the following three questions, you may be a client who tends to micromanage to such a degree that an estate liquidator will not want to take on your project.

1. Have you compiled an inventory listing every single object in the house down to the pots and pans in the kitchen?
2. Have you already researched the worth of over 50 percent of the objects in your home?
3. Have you taken two weeks off from work so that you can work side by side with the estate liquidator and make absolutely sure that they do the right job?

If you answered yes to any of the previous questions, then I sincerely applaud you. Process and outcomes are important to you. Your actions, while extreme to some, do come from a profound desire to have the job done well and correctly. But you are going to have a difficult time getting an estate liquidator to assist you.

LITTLE OR NO STREET PARKING

Estate sales are popular. They can attract hundreds of people over the course of a two- or three-day estate sale, so having parking available is important to the success of it. If there is no place to park, shoppers will turn around and drive away. If an estate liquidator comes to your home built on the side of a hill along a twisting winding mountainous road with no parking, it's possible they may decline your sale. In the past, I have successfully conducted estate sales where there was almost no street parking. It is not impossible, but it does require some creativity.

FAMILY SQUABBLES

Settle your family's differences of opinion about what to do with the stuff before calling an estate liquidator. Your life will be infinitely easier if you do this first. It is best for everyone in a family to be on the same page about whether or not the estate's personal property should be retained or sold via estate sales or at an auction. Estate liquidators can, to some extent, mediate minor issues between family members, but it should be understood by you that they are not trained mediators.

The estate sale tension: You want the most income and buyers want the best deals. Price your items between these extremes and your sale will be successful.

> *Settle your family's differences of opinion about what to do with the stuff before calling an estate liquidator. Your life will be infinitely easier.*

The entire sales process for everyone will move ahead more smoothly where there is accord rather than where there is discord. The how of this, the settling of this type of situation in families where there is rancor or hostility, is difficult and sometimes requires legal assistance.

Problem: Family squabbles.

Solution: Once all the issues in a family about who should get what have been settled, there may still be some disagreements about the best way to sell the estate's remaining personal property. Some family members might think that an auction is a better choice than an estate sale, and they may be right about that. Information about and a procedural understanding of the estate liquidation process is key to resolving most negative issues that come up in families about what is best to do. Have family members read this book or seek out other sources of information about estate sales or estate liquidation.

NO PROOF THAT CLIENT HAS LEGAL AUTHORITY

It is important and legally necessary for estate liquidators to know with certainty that the parties that they are entering into a contract with are legally entitled to act on behalf of the estates they say they represent. So don't be surprised if you are asked to provide court or trust documents that prove you are the executor or trustee for the estate.

Problem: No proof client has legal authority.

Solution: Meet with your attorney and ask that they provide you with documentation proving that you are the estate's legal representative.

TOO HIGH OF AN EXPECTATION ABOUT VALUES

If you think everything in your house is worth significantly more than the estate liquidator who you are interviewing does, chances are there are one of two things happening: Either your expectations are too high given the realities

From half-empty perfume bottles to VHS tapes, which may seem obsolete to many with the advancement of DVD players and Blu-Rays, if you have it, people will buy it.

of the marketplace within your geographical area, or the estate liquidator is inexperienced.

Fair market value is an elusive ideal to attain. The concept of fair market value is not so hard to understand, though; it is what a buyer with cash in hand is willing to pay at a specific period of time for a specific thing. You or someone you hire is presented with an object, a little research is done, and it is found that someone somewhere states that the value of your object is $1,000. Everyone gets this, but what they don't always get is that this is still an abstracted idea about value. There are many nuances that still need to be gleaned from the information that was found. Are the two items actually identical? Are there any variances? Where was the item being offered for sale? Was it for sale on Park Avenue in Manhattan or on Main Street of your hometown? Where an item is being sold has a great deal to do with how much that item can be perceived as being worth to the buying public.

An estate sale is neither the best place to receive the highest value nor is it the worst place; estate sales are where you can reasonably expect that your items will sell for someplace in the middle of the market. In other words, if it is valued at $1,000 on Park Avenue and $500 in a small store on Main Street, you may reasonably expect your item to sell for between $400 and $700 at an estate sale.

CLIENT REJECTS ESTATE LIQUIDATORS FEES AND COMMISSIONS

The single biggest mistake that you as an executor can make is to shop for the services of an estate liquidator based solely upon their fees and commissions. Fees vary depending on the part of the country an estate liquidator is conducting their business, but in general, they range from between 25 percent and 35 percent of the total estate sales income.

If services are equal, higher commissions mean you make less money			
Fee:	Income	Estate Portion	Commission
25%	$10,000	$7,500	$2,500
35%	$10,000	$6,500	$3,500

When you look at the chart on the previous page, there is a $1,000 difference in commissions to an estate liquidator between a 25 percent fee and a 35 percent fee on a $10,000 estate sale.

BUT REMEMBER THE OLD ADAGE: YOU GET WHAT YOU PAY FOR.

The four questions to ask about these two differences in commission structures are:

1. Does a higher fee mean an enhanced service?
2. Will a higher fee correlate to a higher sales income?
3. What are the differences in research and marketing styles?
4. How will different research and marketing styles generate more sales?

If Better Service Means Higher Incomes				
Fee:	Income	Income Enhancement	Estate Portion	Commission
25%	$10,000	None	$7,500	$2,500
35%	$13,500	Extra $3,500	$9,225	$4,275

HIGHER COMMISSIONS GENERALLY MEAN HIGHER INCOMES. Here is why: The more effort that an estate liquidator puts into setting up, pricing, and staffing your sale, the higher incomes that your estate sale can be expected to generate. This is because they have a better capacity to accomplish these five actions:

1. Research.
2. Give more time to set up.
3. Manage sales better by keeping them well staffed.
4. Accept credit cards, which increases sales.
5. Have stronger internet marketing tools.

The better informed they are about your items because they have spent the time to do the right research means that they can sell your estate items for higher prices. A clean, well-organized home attracts a higher caliber of shopper. When an estate liquidator spends the time to really set a home up for an estate sale and has staff on hand to continually bring order to the house during the sale, they are giving greater impetus to their estate sales shoppers to stay longer and spend more money. Accepting credit cards definitely increases sales, but the acceptance of a credit card means that the estate liquidator has to absorb processing fees. Top-flight estate liquidators spend more time on internet marketing, which increases the market reach of your estate sale.

If you decide you're courageous enough to conduct your own estate sale, follow the advice in this chapter carefully and you'll have success.

SHOULD YOU DO YOUR OWN ESTATE SALE?

All across this great country and on just about any given weekend, rain or shine, someone is staging or conducting an estate sale, from highly competent estate sales professionals to mom and pop or family efforts, with each one selling off the household accumulations of many years.

Personally, I think you should hire a professional to conduct your estate sale. Most of you will be entirely out of your knowledge and comfort zones if you try to do this on your own. But I get that not everyone has an estate with high enough dollar values to attract the services or interest of professionals, so people are often left to stage their own estate sales without much recourse or access to any well thought out estate sales setup information.

Here is an expanded and revised upon ten-step guide I wrote for people who cannot, for whatever reason, find an estate sales company to stage a sale for them and have to do it themselves. I wrote it because I became concerned that too many people without the right information were making costly mistakes,

DO YOUR OWN ESTATE SALE IF:

• You have a low or modestly valued estate (less than $5,000).

• There are no competent professionals in your area.

• A professional appraisal has been made and you are certain of values.

NEVER, OR ALMOST NEVER, DO YOUR OWN ESTATE SALE IF:

• You are trying to save money.

• You do not handle confusion, crowds, or rudeness well.

• You are sentimentally attached to the items you are selling.

HIRE A PROFESSIONAL TO CONDUCT YOUR ESTATE SALE WHEN:

• There are high value items needing expert research and marketing.

• Your estate sale needs extensive organization.

• You simply do not have the time.

selling their grandparents' heirlooms and such, for way too little.

A good estate sales professional, one with experience and verifiable references, is more than worth their weight in gold. They and their teams will vastly improve an estate's ability to capture higher dollar incomes via the sale of almost anything that can be found in a home. They know how to do this. The more money they make for you, the more they make for themselves. They are highly motivated because of ethics, and commissions, to do well. Their efforts on behalf of your estate and the greater incomes they will generate will more than offset and pay for the fees of their service.

PLEASE USE THE FOLLOWING GUIDE ONLY IF YOU CANNOT FIND LOCAL ESTATE SALES PROFESSIONALS TO TAKE ON YOUR PROJECT.

TEN-STEP DO-IT-YOURSELF ESTATE SALES GUIDE

STEP 1: ▶ ESTATE SALES ARE PART TRANSITION/PART COUNSELING

Prepare to be surprised …

EXECUTORS: You are about to enter into someone else's private life. Other than the experience of it, nothing else will really prepare you for this task. If you feel that you are being intrusive into someone else's personal life, this is normal. You are going behind the veil of privacy that we all put up between what is most private about us and the way we present ourselves to the world.

You will be learning things about the decedent you never knew and you may also learn things about them you wish you never had. A home is a person's private retreat. Many things are stored and hidden within them that were never meant to be analyzed, viewed, or thought about by others. When dealing with the personal effects of someone who has passed away, a lot comes to the surface, including their relationships to other heirs, as well as other complex relationships they had between siblings, spouses, and their friends.

• •

A good estate sales professional with experience is worth their weight in gold. They will vastly improve an estate's ability to capture higher dollar incomes via the sale of almost anything in a home.

• •

HEIRS AND FAMILY MEMBERS: It is best to remember that difficult family members or friends are attempting to work out issues they've always tried to work out, that this effort to resolve what has been eating away at them does not stop at the passing of a loved one, but continues. As difficult as this can be for all concerned, it's perfectly natural that people will be people. In order for you to get through this, you will need to stay disengaged from their old issues. Only they themselves can work through them. Keep yourself focused on the present task at hand.

REMEMBER TO BREATHE: You are doing something you have not been trained to do and you are going to do the best you can. Take your time. Do your homework. Call in outside help. There is no perfect way to do what has to be done. You will make some mistakes that will have to be okay. Study this book and take notes. Think and think again. This is an emotional time for everyone. If the decisions you are going to be making about what to do with the personal property are made via your emotions, then you may suffer. Try to minimize your emotions to the extent that you can. Keep your eyes open. Stay willing to learn.

PERSONAL PROPERTY IS STICKY: A person is not their stuff, although they are often remembered by it, but people are people and stuff is stuff. Part of your job as the executor is to find ways to delink the emotional human need to create connections between people and things, but it's normal to link people to things. Dad had a watch, but dad was not his watch. Mom had a diamond ring, but mom was not her diamond ring. Grandmother had a set of Limoge china, but grandmother was not her Limoge china. Our loved ones are not the things they owned. They are what is cared about and carried in the heart of our memories.

STEP 2: ▶ START AT THE BEGINNING

SECURE ALL PERSONAL PAPERS: Houses are filled with more personal paper than might at first be imagined. And it is true that some people, perhaps because they are disorganized, will have placed their stock certificates, savings bonds, or their latest will into one or more of their overflowing boxes of personal papers. You'll have to look through these carefully.

- Ask your attorney or accountant to inform you which papers you should be on the lookout for.
- It is best to remove these papers from the premises for safekeeping.
- Especially be on the lookout for documents containing Social Security or credit card numbers or any other financial institutions account numbers.

SEARCH FOR HIDDEN WEALTH: People are clever when they hide their money, silver, jewelry, firearms or other valuables. Remember their intention was to place their valuables far out of reach. For peace of mind, spend a good amount of time on this and do a complete and thorough search of the house.

We have found every conceivable kind of valuable, from envelopes stuffed with cash to misplaced boxes of jewelry, hidden in the strangest places. It is important for you to make a thorough search of the home for firearms or other valuables before turning it over to an estate liquidator, auctioneer, hauler, or, if you are doing your own estate sale, the public.

MAKE THE HOUSE READY FOR HEIRS: If there are other heirs who have some discretion over the contents of the home, do some preliminary layout and arrangement of the contents to make their viewing process easier. Do this only for people who are named in the will. Sometimes within families there are groups or factions who will attempt to influence you. If this is the case, try to do the initial sorting process yourself. Making the house ready for heirs is an important step. One of the last things you want to see happen is for your entire family to hit the once tranquil and peaceful family home and turn it inside out like a tsunami. So be organized and do some preliminary sorting and arranging of the house's contents to make their efforts to see what's there proceed more smoothly.

PRE-ESTABLISH SOME PERSONAL PROPERTY DISBURSEMENT STRATEGIES: It will be most helpful to work out your distribution strategies before other heirs arrive. This is best done in accordance with the conditions of the will. If you have an estate where the contents of the home have not been directly willed to specific family members, then I suggest that you consult with your attorney, who hopefully will help you develop a distribution strategy that will be satisfactory to all.

You want to make sure you have a plan in place before other heirs arrive. It's best if the plan is written out, and fits in with the intentions or the stated will of the decedent. Deviations from the decedent's wishes will need to have been arrived at via consultation with your attorney or other principal heirs who are named in the will. You want to make sure that all interested parties are notified about your distribution strategies in a timely fashion; hopefully before they ever arrive to the family home.

If the will does not clearly state who gets what and instead states, "All of my personal property is to be divided evenly between my children," then you are most definitely going to need to develop some creative disbursement strategies, especially if more than one heir wants the same thing.

DON'T THROW AWAY STUFF OR DONATE IT TOO QUICKLY: I can't overstate or emphasize this enough: It is advisable that you have expert outside assistance to help you determine what items might be donated or thrown away. It is our experience that people will throw away or donate valuable items because they lack the knowledge to fully comprehend what has value and what does not.

STEP 3: ESTATE SALES SETUP AND SUPPLIES LIST

THINK: "How can I attractively set this house up for an estate sale so that everything is displayed and easily seen?" If shoppers can't see it, they can't buy it.

- Remove items from drawers, closets, and cabinets and display neatly on card tables.
- Place fabrics, towels and linens in boxes placed under card tables to save space.
- Group similar items together: China with china, glassware with glassware and so on.
- To prevent theft, place all high-value items in one room; in locked glass cases is best.
- Resist staging items on top of the furniture. This will make furniture sales easier.
- Remember your own personal life and your schedules.
- Give yourself plenty of time.

HERE ARE THE THINGS THAT YOU WILL NEED TO STAGE AND CONDUCT YOUR OWN ESTATE SALE:

- Card tables or banquet tables
- Price stickers, and other adhesive labels
- String tags
- Permanent markers
- Thumbtacks
- Silver polish
- Printed price lists
- Printed directional signs
- Small tool kit
- Packing paper
- Boxes
- Plastic or paper shopping bags
- Garbage bags
- Calculators
- Money belt or cash box
- Yellow caution tape
- Sealable bags for loose items
- Masking tape for pricing fabrics
- Receipt books
- Glass display cases for higher-value items
- Pencils for pricing books
- Notepads
- Aprons
- Name tags

STEP 4: ESTATE SALES PRICING

Now it's time to start pricing your items. To make this easier, first separate high-value items or items whose value you don't completely understand, away from everything else. Price only what you know how to price.

To price higher-value items, it is advisable for you to seek out some expert advice. You may be surprised to find that some items you thought were worthless have high hidden values.

When setting up the merchandise to sell at your estate sale, it makes sense to group like items together, such as porcelain with porcelain ...

And glass with glass.

Card or banquet tables, boxes, calculators, and price stickers are among the important items you'll need to stage your sale.

IMPORTANT REMINDERS:

- When in doubt about pricing, call an estate sales professional in your area (do this even if you think you already know).
- Use guide books, but only for guidance, not as an official means for establishing antiques and collectibles values.
- Be prepared by writing a list of questions to ask an expert about values.
- Always call an appraiser for information about high value antiques and collectibles.
- Use the internet.
- Price your estate sales items using only dollar, fifty cent, or twenty-five cent increments.
- Make sure to price all items that are being offered for sale, as this will save a lot of time at checkout.

Use appraisers, antiques and collectibles price guides or both. There are good antiques and collectibles price guides available from your local book dealer and at krausebooks.com. The internet can also provide you with a wealth of information.

STEP 5: ▶ DETERMINE ESTATE SALES STAFFING

When deciding how many people you will need to staff your estate sale, first determine the layout of the house and its traffic patterns. Ask yourself how will people move through this house during the estate sale? Take this into consideration when thinking about how many people you will need to help you. For a two- or three-bedroom home, we typically will use three to four staff people. Under no circumstances should you do your estate sale solely by yourself. You will definitely need help from family or friends. If possible, have someone stationed in each room of the house during the sale; if this is not possible, then station people by areas or zones within the home. This will make your estate sale more secure and it will proceed more efficiently.

HERE'S THE WAY WE STAFF OUR ESTATE SALES:
• Cashier
• Assistant cashier
• Someone to staff our glass cases and watch over valuables
• One to two staff members to supervise the rest of the house

STEP 6: ▶ ESTATE SALES SCHEDULING AND ADVERTISING

HERE IS A CHECKLIST AND A FEW SUGGESTIONS:
• Set your estate sales date for a weekend.
• We advise that you conduct your estate sale over the course of at least two days.
• Write your ad copy.
• Make sure your ad contains a description of your best items.
• Check for local newspaper classified ad insertion deadlines.
• Place your estate sales ad in the largest newspaper in your metropolitan area.
• Most definitely post an ad on Craigslist or estatesales.net or estatesales.org.
• Post flyers on local Laundromats and coffee shop bulletin boards.
• On the days of your estate sale, make sure you publicly post directional signs along roadways in order to direct buyers to your sale.

STEP 7: ▶ SALES DAY STRATEGIES

As soon as your estate sales ad hits the newspapers or Craigslist, shoppers will instantly know that your sale is a privately run, non-professionally staged estate sale. They will begin attempting to contact you quickly. They are looking to score before anyone else has the chance to shop your sale. Being inundated with "early birds" knocking at your door within hours of your ad hitting the streets is normal. Our best advice is no matter what they say, do not let them in until the actual start date and time of your sale.

Early birds only want to buy your best stuff. They don't care about anything else except making a score. If you allow them to shop your sale early, you will hurt your overall sales success and your sale will instantly become less exciting. One of the key ingredients to make an estate sale successful is shopping frenzy. This is the kind of energy that gets created by shoppers who are seeing many interesting things. If early birds have already bought your estate's best items the day before, you won't be able to create this sort of energy on the days of your sale. Worse than that is if you allow sales to early birds, that information will travel as fast as a wildfire, which will have the negative impact of causing many shoppers to avoid your sale because it has already been picked over.

• •

Remember: Let the best sell the rest. If you sold your best the night before to an early bird, you won't have the best left in your sale to excite your shoppers.

• •

Don't believe their sob stories about how they can't possibly make it the day of your sale because they are traveling out of town or whatever other story they make up to get into your place early. Also don't think you can sell to them in secret the night before the sale and they will keep your confidence about this because they won't. They will tell their buddies and their buddies will tell their friends as soon as they can.

A properly organized estate sale containing at least a few treasures that has been advertised well can expect between 150 to 500 shoppers to visit over the course of the sale. That's a lot of people, so please be ready. Prepare yourself emotionally for the public. They will come from every socio-economic walk of life and their values may not be your values. Remember they had no relationship to the decedent, and their actions, questions, and behaviors may seem disrespectful; expect that this will be the case.

There are three categories of items that might remain in a house after an estate sale:

1. ITEMS THAT STILL HAVE VALUE: For a variety of reasons, there may be items remaining after an estate sale that will still have value. Your choices for what to do with these items are:

• You could decide to keep these remaining items.
• Sell your estate's remaining items as one lot to a dealer.
• Send remaining items of value to a local auction.

If you decide to send your remaining items of value to an auction, please make sure that you first create an auction inventory sheet. This will help you keep track of the items you sent to them.

2. ITEMS THAT CAN'T BE SOLD BUT CAN BE DONATED: After the dust has settled from your estate sale, you will notice that there are leftover items that couldn't be sold but that still have utility. These are the kinds of items that weren't good enough to sell to a remainders' dealer or to send to an auction. But because they are still useful, it is a good idea to donate them to one of many local charities. This is not just a feel-good deed; it also saves money on debris removal cost.

NOTE: If you decide not to have an estate sale and choose instead to donate the estate's contents, make sure you check with your attorney to see if you need

ESTATE SALES MORNING CHECKLIST
• Put street signs up to direct the public to your estate sale.
• Check out the house and make any final adjustments.
• Set up your cashier's table.
• Make sure you have cleared paths through your house to prevent injury or harm.
• Make sure you have a single door that you use both as an entrance and exit.
• Lock all other doors and place "no exit" signs on them.
• Centralize all of your estate sales packing supplies near the cashier for easy and quick checkout.

to have a written certified appraisal generated for estate tax purposes. Make sure your appraiser also adequately answers this question for you, though: "Are there any items I am contemplating the donation of that has significant hidden value?"

3. ITEMS THAT CAN NEITHER BE SOLD NOR DONATED: We call these items debris.

STEP 9: ▶ DEBRIS REMOVAL

This is one of the hardest elements of staging your own estate sale: what to do with the junk stuff that remains. If it could not be sold or donated, then what remains, for all intents and purposes, is best thought of in one of two ways: Material that must be removed to a landfill; or material that may be recycled.

THE EASY WAY: Treat as debris.

• Rent a curbside debris box and fill it.
• Rent a truck and transport debris to a landfill.
• Hire haulers to do the work for you.

THE HARDER WAY: Treat as debris and as recyclables.

• Separate items that can be recycled from those items that are pure trash.
• Transport recyclables to a recycling station.
• Some recyclables have financial value, especially iron, copper, and aluminum, so check on this. You may need to call in a metal scrapper if you have significant amounts of this type of material.
• Whatever remains after your recycling efforts is debris that can either be hauled to the landfill, or placed into a debris box that you've had delivered to your home for this purpose.

STEP 10: ▶ FINAL ESTATE SALES ACCOUNTING

It is likely that you have already opened a bank account in the name of the estate you represent. If you haven't, ask your attorney what sort of documentation you will need to bring with you to the bank in order to accomplish this. To stay on the up and up, you will want to deposit your receipts from your sale into the bank under the name of the estate that you represent.

GREAT ESTATE SALES RECORDS = FEWER DISPUTES WITH HEIRS!

• Keep a log of all of your expenses.

• As you sell an item, write that item's sales information into a log or a receipt book.

• At the end of the estate sale, transcribe your handwritten logs or receipt books into an Excel spreadsheet.

PLEASE NOTE: Because laws vary from state to state, these 10 Steps to Running Your Own Estate Sale are meant solely as a guide and are in no way meant to replace sound legal advice, which you should seek from your attorney.

Here Katherine Codina of Fine Estate Liquidation demonstrates how we use locked glass cases to secure valuables at an estate sale.

Chapter 11

....

SO YOU WANT TO BE IN THE ESTATE SALES BUSINESS

I ONCE PUBLISHED the *Ten-Step Estate Sales Guide* featured in Chapter 10 online, with the good intention of teaching people, who were facing the job of emptying a loved one's home alone, without a clue about what to do.

I was an estate liquidator working in the San Francisco Bay Area and I had written about estate sales, antiques, and collectibles on a blog I had created. One of the results that came from the articles I wrote was that readers from across the country would call or email me looking for more information. I noticed by talking to these people about how to effectively conduct an estate sale that there was almost no written information out there.

To me that meant that people and the estates they represented were kind of floating on a vast expanse of sea, with barely a boat and no paddle. People were making mistakes and I didn't like that. I know, I thought, I will write a free Do It Yourself Estate Sales Guide, stick it up on the Internet, and solve two pressing problems. Now people will know how to do their own estate sale, and I won't have to answer so many emails or phone calls about estates that are completely out of my service area.

These folks weren't getting the help they needed and because of that, they were probably being unduly taken advantage of. The people who were contacting me had estates that were too small for professionals to be able to afford to stage and conduct for them. It seems that there were lots of people in this boat, who could not get access to professional services because of modest values. So, I was pleased with my knight in shining armor effort for being so considerate as to publish a free guide for them. Problem solved, right?

But a funny thing happened on my way to doing something nice for people who couldn't afford the services of professional estate liquidators. And what that was that now that I had created a modest blueprint for how someone might stage and conduct a sale for their little estate, the overwhelming majority of people who began to contact me were those who wanted to get into the estate sales business. Oh my, talk about unintended consequences.

I had intended the guide to be used by just plain folks to give them an outline of the whole estate sales process. I wanted families to have the necessary tools to help them through the quagmire and chaos that regularly occurs at an estate sale. I was mainly motivated by the belief that if these people used the guide, it wouldn't really matter that they hadn't been able to get the attention of professionals because, having read it, these folks would have a measure of protection.

Shortly after I made the free guide available in 2007, the economy took its epic turn for the worse, causing many people to lose their jobs, look for others, and even contemplate new careers. So it made perfect sense that some of these people started to look at starting their own estate liquidation companies. I'm betting that thousands of them decided to try this. I think many of them thought that it was going to be easy, that all they had to do was print up some business cards, create a little website, make some phone calls, and then sit back and watch as people who needed this service beat a path to their door.

But they were living in a fairy-tale world. They wanted to believe that what an estate liquidator does is easy. They didn't know that the specific skills and knowledge that are required of an estate liquidator only comes to a professional after many years of successes and failures. Starting an estate liquidation company is not a sure and easy path to fame, adulation, or buckets of cash. Starting an estate liquidation company is not easy, nor will it necessarily be profitable. To be profitable, you need great ethics, a wonderful staff, and more than just a little bit of luck; you have to be willing to take on the business in such a way that it becomes a part of your lifestyle.

....

Starting an estate liquidation company is not easy, nor will it necessarily be profitable. To be profitable, you need great ethics, a wonderful staff, and more than a bit of luck; you have to be willing to take on the business in such a way that it becomes a part of your lifestyle.

....

As time went by, the source of the calls and emails shifted almost entirely from people who needed information about how to conduct their own estate sale, to people who wanted to start an estate sales business. Big shift. The people who called wanted to know all sorts of curious things like: How do you get your clients? Do I need a license? Do I need to be insured? Could you please send me a copy of the contract that you use? I even had people who were a bit more sincere, who offered to hire me as a consultant, and teach them how to get into the business.

I was patient, took their calls, and answered their emails. I gave them the best thing any professional can give to someone in need of information—my time. I can't say that I didn't sometimes resent it just a little bit. I have no real

The author and his wife, Valetta, on the next page, spend a lot of time researching objects to get the best value they can for their clients.

way of knowing how many estate sales companies were first started by people who read my online guide. I shudder a bit to think how many might have.

It takes way more than just a desire to make money to get ahead and to prosper in the estate sales business. To be of any assistance to the people who need the services of an estate liquidator, you need to know a great deal. Way more than any free estate sales guide has any chance of teaching someone.

THE ESTATE SALES BUSINESS IS ONE OF THE MOST COMPLEX JOBS IN THE WORLD

Okay, so it's not rocket science, but it is complex. You have two bosses. Your first boss is the client whose estate you are working on, and your second boss is the customer who is shopping and looking for the best deal they can get at your client's house. Now, over a beer at a company picnic, these two people would probably really like each other, but in the arena of an estate sale, these two parties have opposing goals. The client wants the most amount of money. The customer wants to pay the least amount of money. Between them is a pockmarked minefield of dashed hopes and dreams.

Every single house you go into is different and each has different kinds of stuff. One person collects paintings. Are they oil paintings or watercolors? How will you ever learn to tell the difference between a drawing and a print? In another person's house, they collected trains, so now you have to learn the difference between gauge and scale or Marklin and Lionel.

If you think that all you have to do is figure the above out, wait—it gets worse; you're just beginning.

YOUR MOST IMPORTANT TOOL IS TO CARE

If you don't care about people's problems, then you'll never get to solve them. It's as simple as that. My one guiding principle is the knowledge that stuff is not just stuff, that what I find in a home once belonged to a human being and that human being deserves my respect, as well as my attention.

We have all heard the metaphor that a person's home is his castle. So many things happen in a home. Good things and bad things; the major milestones and events that have been realized and celebrated at dinner tables; the intimacy of the bedroom; the laughter of every celebration; the tears of every family failure or rejection. The home is a place of refuge, for alone time, as well as a place to repair from the lonely times. This is the place that you have been invited into.

So, it's not about the stuff. It's not about the treasures. It's not about how much money you're going to make. It's not even about your client's satisfaction. It's about grace. It's about honor. It's about respect. When you can internalize and make this list a part of your ethic, then look for the treasure, the cash, the revenues you might generate.

If you approach it any differently than this, you're just a dealer, or somebody only looking to make money, and that's okay. Just know that when you sit across from a potential client in their loved one's home explaining your services, that no matter what you say, or how you say it, they will know you really only care about yourself.

If you don't really care about the humanness of the space you have entered into, you'll only ever have a job. Not a passion. Not a profession. It's all about the caring that leads you to strive to learn your way through the great many personal and technical challenges that exist each day in the estate liquidation business. If you don't presently care and don't want to learn how to care in the near future, do yourself a great favor—either don't start in this business, or if you have already, quit.

I remember three years ago I was called into a beautiful house on a hillside overlooking the picturesque town of Sausalito, California. Of course I was excited; Sausalito is a wealthy town and this house was likely to have some expensive stuff in it; surprises and treasures.

The man who called me lived somewhere in the South, and he'd come to take care of his dying friend. I didn't know this on my drive over to meet with him. In fact, I almost never know much of the story until I knock on the door and I am allowed entry. This was going to be one of those rare circumstances where, soon after being invited in, I would learned there was a man in the master bedroom, dying. His name was Jim. He was the man of the house, had spent many a fine year living there enjoying his possessions, using his silver and china, entertaining his guest, family, and friends. And now he was in a back bedroom waiting to pass from this world into the next.

Before you think how morbid this all sounds, Jim's friend called me with his full knowledge and permission. The friend was not greedy to sell the stuff; in fact, he stood to gain nothing of monetary value because Jim was donating everything to charity.

I was introduced to Jim and I can't say I really knew how to talk to a dying stranger, but I did the best I could. I discovered that earlier that day, another estate liquidator had also visited, looked the house over, and given his pitch for why his company was the right company to conduct an estate sale for this project.

I know the man who runs that estate company. He's a great guy, extraordinarily knowledgeable, and personable. I don't know if he cared or didn't care about Jim. I never asked him, but my guess is that he probably did. But what he did not do was care about the entire situation. You have to see yourself as someone there to work on behalf of the expressed wishes of the person who owned the house and lived there. You have to stay in touch with the humanity of the dying man and can't ignore it.

My company did get that job and we were chosen over the other estate liquidation company because we saw the whole picture and understood not just the value of the objects in the home, which of course we noticed, but also because we demonstrated while speaking to Jim and his friend, that we would care, honor, and respect his home.

NO ONE KNOWS EVERYTHING

Get over yourself. No one can know everything about antiques and collectibles. The best skill that you should make every effort to acquire is the skill of learning how to know when you don't know. It is no proof of a deficit of acumen to admit to a client that you don't know what something is or what it's worth.

In any house, there are hundreds of categories of things to look at, to understand, and to append values to. Within the hundreds of categories of things you might get to find in a house are thousands of sub-categories. For instance, let's look at the category of fine china.

My one guiding principle is the knowledge that stuff is not just stuff, that what I find in a home once belonged to a human being and that human being deserves my respect, as well as my attention.

Fine china is the main category. What type of fine china it is, where it was made, what pattern it is, and who made it are each separate subcategories of the category fine china. It would take years to become a specialist in fine china.

Of the category of fine china and its hundreds of subcategories, there are hundreds of questions you'll

It would take years to become a specialist of fine china or its hundreds of subcategories, but it's possible, in a shorter time, to develop a general knowledge of it.

have to learn to answer in order to properly appraise the item of fine china that you're looking at. What is china, anyway? Well, it turns out that china is not just a main category in and of itself; it is also a subcategory of tableware. There is an incredible amount to learn about tableware because now that we've opened that up as a category, we find that tableware is a large and vast category of items that are utilized to serve and present food.

By extrapolation, having to know everything that there is to know or that there might be to know about fine china would be difficult, especially when you add to that expertise the need to know how to be an expert in the valuing of all the other categories you might find in the home. And china is but one category. Daunting, isn't it?

· ·

It was like I had shot a starter pistol to signal the beginning of a race, to judge from the stampede and mad dash of shoppers from the garden entrance gate to the front door of the house. First lesson: Crowd control is important.

· ·

When I first started in the estate sales business, I was understandably nervous about meeting with clients, knowing that they would ask me questions about items in their home that I wouldn't have the foggiest notion about. I thought that a professional had to instantly show the ability to not only give a value to any item that a house might contain, but that they also should know the item's history and any other backstory there might be about whatever the item was. I would get all twisted up about this. I dreaded the meeting. I thought any gap in my knowledge would be noticed as a professional deficit and would prove, by extension, that my services were less than comprehensive and would make me look foolish. Inept.

The flipside of wanting to look like an expert to my clients was the horror that I might look like an inexperienced buffoon to the customers who were shopping my estate sales. When I first began in the business, because I was just learning about what stuff was and how much it was worth, word spread quickly that there was a new guy in town who didn't know what the items he was selling were worth and was pricing them cheaply. No one told me this, of course, but what I got from my customers were knowing smiles, as they stood patiently in line to get into my sale and pick me mercilessly. Oh well, we all have to learn some way.

MY FIRST SALE: I KNEW NOTHING

I remember the first estate sale I ever conducted over 17 years ago, as if it were yesterday. I lived in a small town in northern California and a friend who knew that I wanted to get into the estate sales business referred me to a woman whose mom had recently passed away. The daughter I was to meet had laid large plastic tarps down onto the front lawn of her mom's house and then placed the entire contents of her house on top of them. Everything this woman's mom had ever owned was now on the front lawn.

The daughter did this because she didn't see that there was much value to her mom's things, not at least in comparison to the value of the house, which she needed to fix up and make ready for sale. To do that, she had convinced herself she needed the house to be empty. When I got there, we pulled back the tarps and I got my first chance to see all the varied things that her mom had once owned. This was my first experience as a liquidator and because I had not yet developed a good understanding of how to pick my way through layers of personal property and determine if there was enough there to do an estate sale, I almost did not accept the job. It looked just like stuff to me, too.

But I persevered. I had to learn, after all, and needed to gain the experience, so we wrote up a contract and both signed it. Together with a partner, we brought everything back into the home, priced it all as best as we could, and staged it attractively. I put a small ad in the local newspaper, went home, and waited for the first day of the sale.

· ·

My prices were so cheap, my customers came
up to me at checkout with armloads of stuff.
Second lesson: Learn to price.

· ·

On Saturday morning, as I drove up to the sale, I noted that there were many more cars on the street than usual and as the house came into view, I saw a throng of about 75 people. This was going to be interesting, I thought. I didn't know better, so I assumed it would be perfectly okay to let everyone in all it once, so I did. It was like I had shot a starter pistol to signal the beginning of a race, to judge from the stampede and mad dash of shoppers from the garden entrance gate, to the front door of the house. First lesson: Crowd control is important.

It was a free-for-all circus and the word pandemonium comes to mind. I had unwittingly allowed the sale to devolve into sheer chaos. Because hindsight is 20/20, suffice it to say I never allowed that to happen again. As I said, I had

I had a huge line of restless and impatient shoppers all asking for prices for items they were looking to buy. Third lesson: Price everything before opening.

priced everything as best as I could, but really what I had done was to price only the main objects in the house that I thought had value. The rest of the contents I quoted prices to people as they brought them up to me at checkout. Also, my prices were so cheap, my customers came up to me at checkout with armloads of stuff. Second lesson: Learn to price. Within one hour of opening up the sale, I had a huge line of restless and impatient shoppers all asking for prices for items they were looking to buy. Third lesson: Price everything before opening.

Since I knew I didn't really have a clue about what things were worth to properly price them, and even though I was afraid to look foolish, I started asking people who were in line buying items, these questions: "Why are you buying this?" "What is it?" I'm sure I dumbfounded plenty of dealers and pickers that morning, but I had to know. Gathering information about what items were and how much they might be worth had to start somewhere, and in order for me to have success in the estate sales business, I was going to have to continue asking questions every day. Some people were willing to give me information, while others couldn't be bothered. I learned much from both.

I learned that what was worse than not knowing what an item was or its value was someone unwilling to engage themselves in an educational process that would lead them, whether they looked foolish or not, to a greater professionalism. Asking questions leads to a true professionalism.

AT BEST, AN ESTATE LIQUIDATOR IS A COMPETENT GENERALIST

In this business, and after doing it for over 17 years, at best, all I might ever become is the best antiques and collectibles generalist I can. For anyone wanting to get into the business, your overriding single-minded focus has to be on gaining the competency of a high-functioning generalist in the field of antiques and collectibles, and to combine that with gaining the expertise to properly stage and conduct an in-house estate sale. The only real specialty you need to learn is how to become a specialist in the acquisition of knowledge as you need it.

A generalist in the auction world is someone who knows a little about a lot, and a specialist is someone who knows a lot about a little. Most antiques dealers and pickers are generalists. The biggest auction houses send out gener-

It's important to look for maker's marks and any other clues that will help you determine what an object is and its value.

In time, with practice and patience, you will learn how to properly price the wide assortment of personal property that you find in a home.

alists to first appraise an estate. This might seem like a heresy to some appraisers, but most appraisers, be they ASA, ISA or whatever, are generalists. Only specialty appraisers are specialists. As an estate liquidator, to see yourself as a generalist is not a bad thing. Most estate liquidators are generalists. Learn how to be the best one you can.

WHAT MAKES ME A PROFESSIONAL IS MY ABILITY TO:

1. Admit when I don't know.
2. Know an expert who does.
3. Know how to ask the right expert the right questions.

HOW TO OVERCOME YOUR DEFICIT OF KNOWLEDGE

As outlined above, the first way to overcome the fact that an estate liquidator is a generalist and not a specialist is to admit that a generalist does not have the knowledge or informational skills that a specialist has. There's no shame in it. To be a great estate liquidator, you don't have to be a specialist in 10,000 categories of things; you only have to be a specialist in how to acquire the kind of information that will best serve the needs of your clients. That means you have to develop relationships with experts.

HOW TO DEVELOP "THE EYE"

After the experience of my first estate sale and realizing how much I truly did not know, I began exploring the subjects of antiques and collectibles with an almost insatiable zeal. In those days, there was no Internet to speak of, but there were guide books, auction catalogs, and mail order dealer lists. I bought lots of books and old auction catalogs and poured over

My wife, Valetta, with all the tools needed to act as cashier.

Staff member Lesley Papola, carefully entering sales information into a receipt book.

them. My curiosity took over, but I was not that systematic and didn't try to figure it all out. What I did instead was to pursue categories of antiques and collectibles that interested me.

I'd always been fascinated with costume jewelry, so the first book I bought was about that. I read the book cover to cover many times. I best learn by immersing myself in the subject I want to become familiar with, so I also went to flea markets and auctions and examined many pieces of costume jewelry up close. I was just having fun, taking in information, handling jewelry, and talking to people who were dealing in it.

It was a good time and in the process, I got to learn more about costume jewelry than might be possible from only reading books and it wasn't long before I had the ability to buy costume jewelry for a low price and sell it for a higher one. I can safely say that even though I had immersed myself in the subject, I hadn't really become an "expert," but I developed "my eye."

Again, I followed my curiosity and in small ways, I started to learn about antiques and collectibles. I wasn't particularly methodical and did not take copious notes. I certainly did not try to memorize the prices or item descriptions that I read in guidebooks. Instead, I just hung out in the world of stuff and went to antiques stores and estate sales and looked at what people were buying, what they seemed to be so desirous of, and noticed how much they were paying. I figured shoppers knew more about what they were doing, especially the pickers and dealers, than I did. I followed them, listened in on their conversations, and engaged with anyone who I thought might know anything pertinent to my pursuits.

I think my brain might have collapsed into itself if I had approached it in any other manner. I researched only items I thought looked cool and it turns out, at least for me, that by following my curiosity for no other reason than that I liked the way an item looked, this led to the development of a "sense" of what sorts of things needed my attention.

The next category of collectibles to catch my interest was old postcards. I had heard that there was an Alphonse Mucha postcard that had sold for the princely sum of $5,000. This was in 1997 and today it would sell for more. I was completely blown away and had to learn why a small slip of paper, and an old one at that, was so valuable. I wanted to find that postcard or any other postcard that might have a significant value. I looked through box after box of old postcards to no avail, but trying to learn about postcards led me to the fascinating world of ephemera or what is commonly known by the trade as "old paper."

By nurturing an insatiable curiosity, I blundered my way to brilliance. Curiosity is an essential component to understanding the world of antiques and collectibles and gaining the skill enough to have "the eye" for what might have value. There is not an estate liquidator worth their salt who has not needed to rely on this sense. Sometimes it is only because of curiosity that one item or another gets noticed. Curiosity is like sonar sending out a questioning signal that then bounces back: Hey, this thing over here is not like the rest. Pay attention ... separate this ... call a specialist. Trust your gut—this may be an item that has vast income potential.

Any single category of antiques or collectibles quickly leads to information about all of its subsequent subcategories. It's all tangential and interconnected. You really can't talk about or appraise Georgian furnishings without having to learn something about Queen Anne or Regency furnishings, if for no other reason than to understand Georgian furnishings, you need to be able to contrast its style with other time periods.

HOW TO KNOW WHEN YOU DON'T KNOW?

Here's the short answer: You tell yourself the truth and say, "I don't know." Here's a longer answer:

A. Your potential client stares at you in disbelief or you hear their audible snickers when you tell them a long-winded made up story about what one of their items is worth.

B. Your estate sales are cleared out of their best and most valuable items in the first few hours of the sale.

C. You don't seem to want to learn or change your strategies when you experience the above two mistakes.

KNOW WHOM TO ASK

The first person you want to take time to establish a business relationship with is a personal property appraiser, someone who has verifiable credentials and whose expertise will be as a generalist.

You want to make sure that the person you pick for this professional relationship has no interest in acquiring or purchasing items of value from the estates they will be helping you with. They are not there to buy; they are there only to assist you in an appraisal process. You can find personal property appraisers by going to the International Society of Appraisers or the American Society of Appraisers websites and looking for people who are doing business in your area.

Communicate clearly with these professionals that what you want is to establish a working relationship, whereby they will, for a fee, do a "walk through" of your setup estate sale and give you values for the items in the house that you are not sure about. You want this person's general expertise to help you appraise specific items, look the house over, and to make sure you

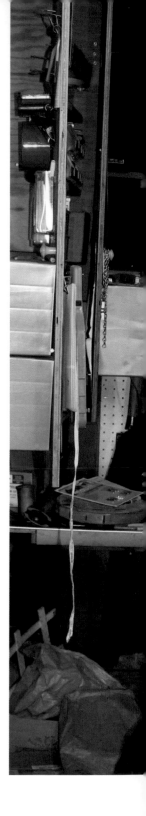

haven't made any mistakes about value or attribution. As you move further into your career as an estate liquidator, you will expand your professional circle of experts and specialists you need on a case-by-case basis. At all cost, avoid the temptation to trade professional services for items found in your client's homes. This blurs the line of what is considered ethical. Your actions on behalf of the estate that you're working with must always be of the highest and most transparent standards.

Even with the reference books I was reading and the estate and auction sales I was attending, I was only able to learn so much. So for the first three or four years I was in business, I always hired a local appraiser affiliated with the International Society of Appraisers to walk through my projects. Her name was Patricia and through her wonderful guidance, I was able to fill in the many gaps in my expertise.

It's true that I've always been drawn to well-made and interesting things and some of that must have contributed to choosing a career in the estate sales business in the first place. I can easily state for the record that even after 17 years of being an estate liquidator, although I have had the great good fortune to acquire several subspecialties, my one and true skill acquired, whether through the dint of luck or hard work, is the competency of a high-functioning generalist who is guided principally by curiosity, with my favorite question being, What is it?

Martin and Valetta Codina.

I suggest that you start a journal and answer the ten questions on P. 254 one by one.

Challenge yourself when answering these questions. Give yourself reasons for and against the idea of starting your own business. Check in with your motivations and don't kid yourself. Tell yourself the truth. If you have never started a business before, make sure that you read all you can about the pitfalls and benefits. Having a business of any kind is not for everyone.

A successful estate liquidation business is hands on, and working ten to twelve hours a day, seven days a week, is more the rule than the exception. If burnout and fatigue are issues in your present job, please realize that the effort that will be required of you to power your estate sales business will seem never ending. The estate liquidation business is a lifestyle business. You better love it because its many facets and responsibilities will take over your life.

If you are thinking of going into this business because you do not have much money, and you think this one will suddenly bring in truckloads of cash, think again. Not only will it take a few years to establish your business, to do so will require some capital.

This is not an easy business to get into. Other estate liquidators won't embrace you, dealers and shoppers will pick you, and of the many other road-blocks to your success, the biggest one that you have to learn your way through is the acquisition of a strong knowledge base about antiques and collectibles.

Making mistakes about what something is worth and selling it for too cheaply is costly, but trust me that you can get through. But making mistakes in regards to your ethics are deadly; there is almost no room for mistakes when it comes to people and their money. Pay your clients. Bad news travels more quickly than good, and that is definitely the case in this business. Do your best. Stay focused and honest. Success happens slowly, not overnight. Hang in there.

It is possible to start an estate sales business. People succeed at this. This is an amazing business with much growth potential. It is an industry that will only get larger. To fuel this growth, many more competent people will enter its ranks. One of them could be you.

Every day, I thank my lucky stars that I have been fortunate enough to find a business that I love, and can remain so faithful to. That I have been able to support myself and my family with this business, and to have been so embraced by the many people in the industry, is one of the greatest gifts I have ever received.

Many estate sales companies are family run businesses. Katherine Codina, the author's wonderful daughter, has been at this since the age of fourteen.

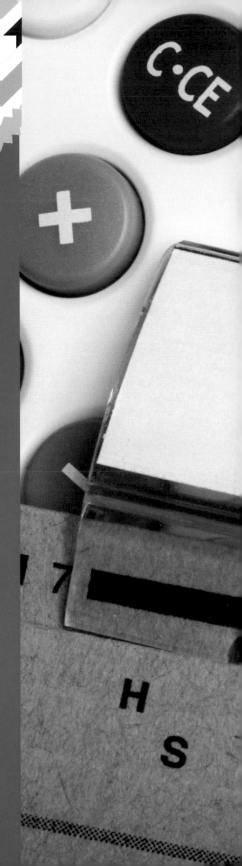

Chapter 12

....

HOW TO INTERVIEW AN ESTATE LIQUIDATOR

TAX+

ON
AC

Estate
Plan

8

9

IJ

Sch

OKAY, STOP! Before you call an estate liquidator and make an appointment with them to do a walkthrough of your estate, you'll need to do some prep work first. If you have the luxury of time, give yourself that time. Take the following seven steps and try not to be in a hurry. Rushing through these steps too fast could have an adverse effect on the positive outcome of your estate sale.

Estate liquidators need clear and thoughtful explanations and directions from you about your goals and expectations, and also need to know precisely which of the many items you will be showing them are actually for sale.

SEVEN PRELIMINARY STEPS TO TAKE BEFORE INTERVIEWING AN ESTATE LIQUIDATOR

STEP 1: DO A THOROUGH SEARCH OF THE HOUSE.

Even though it may seem obvious to many readers that they should do a thorough search of the home before turning over the keys to an estate liquidator, you would be surprised to learn how few people who are faced with the task of taking care of the personal property of an estate really do so.

I can't tell you how many times I have found deeply personal items in a home—items that you wouldn't really want to reveal to perfect strangers. Items of a sexual nature, love letters, compromising photos, tax and financial records, old Social Security cards, and the list goes on. These aren't things you want people outside your family to have.

People hide things. It's just a fact of life. In almost every home I have ever conducted an estate sale, the occupants put the effort into hiding something, whether it was money, gold, jewelry, or coins. Your job as an executor is to protect the privacy, as well as the value, of the estate. So look, and then look again.

Take the time to check under the beds, go through all the drawers and remove them from their dressers and look all around each of them. Open every single box inside the house, taking care to peer inside each of them, and even look under the rugs.

STEP 2: ▶ WRITE A LIST OF THE VALUABLES.

The first reason you should do this is for estate purposes. The second is so that you can keep track of the most important and valuable items in the home.

If you have items of high value and there is any doubt at all about the security of the home, you should definitely consider removing those items until you need to bring them back, either for estate disbursement or to show an estate liquidator.

Having a written list of valuable items will also help your consultations with an estate liquidator go smoothly, as you will be able to refer to your list and assure that the liquidator has been made aware of what is really in the home. An estate liquidator is not a mind reader. They won't know what's valuable in a house if they can't see it or have not been made aware that they are there.

The average estate sale will have several thousand individual items in them, so most estate liquidators will not create a pre-estate sale inventory list; this would take too long. So, it's especially important that you make a list of the highest-valued items in the home, which will help you later when it comes to the final reconciliation of the estate.

Estate liquidators need clear and thoughtful explanations and directions from you about your goals and expectations, and also need to know precisely which of the many items you will be showing them are actually for sale.

STEP 3: ▶ DECIDE WHAT IS AND WHAT IS NOT GOING TO BE PART OF THE ESTATE SALE.

Way before you have an estate liquidator arrive to take a look at your home's contents, you and your family have many decisions to make about what to keep and what to sell.

I have written elsewhere about the free for all that can happen if you get the whole family together for this, and it may devolve into a free-for-all despite your best efforts, but sometimes that's unavoidable.

The one thing that can instantly de-motivate an estate liquidator from working with your estate is for them to walk into a house crammed full of amazing stuff, only to be told that 90 percent of it is being retained by the family. Get real clear about what you or your family is keeping and what you are willing to sell. If possible, remove items that are being retained by the

Though estate liquidators are specialists in managing and conducting on-site public estate sales, that does not mean they are experts in every category of antiques, collectibles, or items of antiquity. If they happen to walk by something that you think has value, do yourself and them a favor and ask them about it.

family before the estate liquidator even gets there. This creates a realistic picture for the estate liquidator to see what the house contains and allows them to quickly ascertain whether or not yours is an estate they can work with.

STEP 4: **REMOVE OR PLACE STICKY NOTES ON ITEMS TO BE RETAINED BY THE FAMILY.**

Now that you have made your key decisions about what will and won't be part of the estate sale, take a little time to affix either a sticky note or even colored labels on the items being retained. It's a good idea to use different colors for each individual family member. Do this especially if you are not going to be able to remove all the items from the home that the family is going to retain before the estate liquidator gets there. This will help you and the liquidator more easily get through the initial walkthrough process. It will also keep all heirs aware of what item has been chosen by another family member.

For purposes of the estate, you as an executor can then go around the house and make a master list of what items have been retained and by which family member.

STEP 5: **PLACE VALUABLES AND ITEMS OF INTEREST IN PLAIN SIGHT SO THAT THEY CAN BE SEEN BY THE ESTATE LIQUIDATION COMPANY'S REPRESENTATIVE.**

Prepare for the day that you will meet with an estate liquidator by making sure that you have made visible all the items that you can think of that may have significant value. Place high-value items in plain sight. Some estate liquidators are busy and even the best of them on any given day may seem brusk or in a hurry. The estate liquidator that you want to choose is the one who finds the time to patiently explain their process and the many ways they can help.

You want to make sure that each estate liquidator you interview has seen all that there is to see because they will make their assessment about whether they can work with your estate based upon what they perceive to be the aggregate value of your estate.

Ideally you want to choose an estate liquidator who exhibits knowledge about a wide variety of items found in your home, from its furnishings to its collectibles.

Little items like these vintage purses, when sold at your estate sale, will add measurable income to its results. The purses shown here have a combined value of at least $1,500.

Though estate liquidators are specialists in managing and conducting on-site public estate sales, that does not mean that they are specialists or experts in every category or subcategory of antiques, collectibles, or items of antiquity. If they happen to walk by something that you think has value, do yourself and them a favor and ask them about it.

STEP 6: ▶ DON'T WORRY IF THE HOUSE IS NOT IN PERFECT ORDER.

One of the biggest reasons you may be avoiding a call to an estate liquidator is that the house you are charged with clearing is a big mess—layers of clutter and years of accumulations are all piled haphazardly everywhere, piles of what you are certain can only be described as dense loads of junk. You may think that no one in his or her right mind would want to deal with it, least of all a professional. But that's what professionals get paid to do. You really don't have clean everything up before calling. Estate liquidators have seen it all, and the best of them will understand. They really are not in the business of judgment, anyway; it's their task to assist you through the mess and toward a solution.

The reason I am making this point is because many of my past clients simply waited way too long to call me and needlessly suffered under the weight of what to do.

Another reason I am suggesting that you not clean it all up before the estate liquidator gets there is because, though you are well meaning, you may inadvertently throw items of value away. Let the person you contract with determine what to throw away. They will be better and more experienced with it.

STEP 7: ▶ PRINT A COPY OF THE 17 QUESTIONS ON P. 267 AND HAVE IT AT THE READY FOR YOUR MEETINGS WITH ESTATE LIQUIDATORS.

You want to make sure that you have ready access to these questions. Check each one off as you ask them.

TIPS: It is helpful to have a separate folder for each estate liquidation company that you are going to interview containing the following:

• List of questions to ask each company
• Pictures of items not presently in the house that you wish to sell
• Notes about the meeting you have with each estate liquidator
• Promotional materials that each company gives you

THE 17 BEST QUESTIONS TO ASK AN ESTATE LIQUIDATOR

It is not just the answers to the questions below that will give you enough information to best determine which estate liquidator to choose for your project, but also how they answer them, which will reveal their demeanor, manners and acumen.

1 IS THERE ENOUGH HERE TO DO AN ESTATE SALE?

It's likely that the person you are interviewing will let you know this even before you get a chance to ask the question, but it is an important question nonetheless. Oftentimes, their answer will reveal just what sort of high or low value estate sale you have, as well as if this particular estate liquidator is the right one for your project.

2 DOES YOUR COMPANY HAVE ROOM ON ITS CALENDAR?

There are a number of important reasons to ask this question and they mostly have to do with whether or not this estate liquidator takes on too many projects at a time or has such an open schedule, they don't have much going on. And you also want to know if their time lines fit in with your time lines.

Ideally, you want an estate liquidator who doesn't take on more than one project a week. Any more than that and it may be an indication that they and their staff are stretched too thin. It's a given that the more time a competent and professional estate liquidator puts into your project, the better the revenue results for your estate sale will be, so make sure they really can fit your project into their schedule.

3 HOW LONG WILL THE ENTIRE ESTATE SALE SET UP PROCESS AND ACTUAL SALE TAKE?

With this one innocent question, you will discover a lot about the methodology of the estate liquidator you are interviewing. How much or how little time they take to set the home up for a sale could let you know how careful or casual they are.

Some estate liquidators literally come into a home at breakneck speed and in a day or two will have an entire house set up. That doesn't mean that they have done it well, though, or that they will have priced most things. It really only means that the house has the appearance of being set up, or that your sale was so small that it really could be set up in such a short time.

Other estate liquidators will take their time, spending as much as several weeks to set up a home, because that is how much time they need to carefully stage a sale, and research the values of the items that they have found there.

Bronze commemoratives, religious items, 10k gold trinket jewelry, and WWII army IDs each have a buyer looking for them at an estate sale.

In the end, it is not about how long an estate liquidator takes to set up and stage a sale, but in how well they use their time doing so. In the time they allot to your sale, will they be able to price at least 90 percent of the items in the home, make the house presentable for an estate sale, and effectively market your sale to as many buyers as possible? And will they be able to accomplish all of this in a time line consistent with the time constraints of the estate's schedule?

4 CAN YOU PLEASE EXPLAIN YOUR COMPANY'S SET-UP AND SALES PROCESS?

It turns out that there are essentially only two ways to set up an estate sale: the simple way, and the complex way. The simple approach is to rearrange the furniture, remove most objects from cupboards and so on, and price only the higher-valued items. The complex approach is to skillfully reorganize the entire house, taking care to set it up in such a fashion that it takes on the appearance of a staged production; all items are then researched and priced. The simple way produces mostly modest results, while the complex way produces and generates the greatest amount of income.

An estate liquidator's answer to this question will let you know how serious and diligent they intend to be about generating a maximum income for you on behalf of your estate.

You'll also want to ask them how they will leave the house post estate sale. Do they leave the house in broom clean condition, or will that be the responsibility of the estate?

• •

Price negotiation is one of the best sales levers an estate liquidator has, and shoppers love to haggle.

• •

5 HOW MANY SHOPPERS DO YOU LET INTO THE HOUSE AT ONE TIME?

Want mayhem in your home? Of course not, but that's what you'll get if you choose a company that doesn't limit the number of shoppers in the home at any one time.

Typically, a professional company will only allow somewhere between fifteen and thirty shoppers in your home at a time. This is important because reasonably limiting the number of shoppers will cut back on or eliminate theft, reduce liability, and creates a calmer shopping atmosphere, which is more easily shopped by buyers and managed by staff.

6 IS YOUR COMPANY INSURED?

Absolutely under no circumstances should you do business with a company that is uninsured, and by that I mean they must carry property damage and public liability insurance in an amount that has a chance of covering any potential losses.

In addition, they should also have a worker's compensation policy in case any of their employees become injured. You want to ask them for definite proof of this insurance and make sure that their policy is a type that covers the sorts of occurrences that may happen during the normal conducting of an estate sale. You'll also need to make sure that your own insurance policy is current because if there were an injury to a person in your home, the shopper may go directly after the estate to make their claim and not the estate liquidation company's insurer. What will then possibly happen is that the estate liquidator's insurance company will enter into settlement negotiations with your insurance company. Either way, by making sure that the company you are wanting to work with has their own insurance and by making sure your own homeowner's policy is in place, you will be acting in a way that is responsible to the entire estate.

7 HOW DOES YOUR COMPANY DETERMINE VALUES?

Given the absolute variety of items that can be found in even an average home, anything from Tupperware to valuable old master paintings, it is incredibly important that the estate liquidator you are going to work with has full access to the best appraising techniques and tools that are available.

There is no single person on the planet who can tell you with certainty what everything in a house is worth, so the estate liquidator that you are interviewing won't know at first glance what the samurai sword your grandfather brought back from the war is worth. Or what the John F. Kennedy signature your mom was lucky enough to collect as a teen is worth. That's what research is for. That's what the estate sales professionals' working relationship with other specialists accomplishes. You also want to determine if the estate liquidator you're speaking with has those sorts of connections and whether or not they subscribe to one of several Internet antiques and collectibles valuation databases.

Guard yourself from working with anyone who says that their best way of determining the value of an item is their experience. If this is their stance and for some reason you are locked into using their services, at least question them about their method.

Books, no matter the subject, and media of all types will enjoy steady sales during your weekend estate sale.

8 DOES YOUR COMPANY NEGOTIATE DISCOUNTS WITH ESTATE SALES CUSTOMERS?

There is not an estate liquidation company anywhere in America that does not discount or in some way negotiate discounts with their customers during a sale. It's all part of the give-and-take of the sales process and is a vital and important means to getting your house empty. Price negotiation is one of the best sales levers an estate liquidator has, and shoppers love to haggle.

What you want to find out, though, is how the liquidator you are interviewing negotiates and what their style is. Most of them have tried-and-true tricks and strategies for dealing with customers who come at them with low-ball offers. You want to be sure that they don't negotiate too much at the beginning and not enough at the end.

So how does the negotiating process work? Essentially at an estate sale, all prices are fixed. They are not like auctions where the beginning bid is often set low and the bidding process hopefully increases the purchase price. At an estate sale, a liquidator will start at the highest price they think their shoppers will pay, and it may surprise you how many shoppers will pay the starting price of the item as marked.

One effective approach to the negotiating process for a three-day estate sale is to not negotiate on the first day; negotiate to some degree, maybe up to 25 percent off, the second day, and then empty the house with a 50 percent off sale the third and final day.

9 HOW DOES YOUR COMPANY ADVERTISE ITS SALES?

Today there are many ways for estate liquidators to market and advertise the estate sales that they are conducting. I'll list these in order of importance:

- Up-to-date email list
- Website posting
- Craigslist or estatesales.net listing
- Directional street signs
- Newspaper classified ad

The best way to let everyone know about an upcoming estate sale is a strong and well-maintained email list. Ask the estate liquidator you're interviewing the following questions: How many people are on your email list? What percentage of the emails sent are actually opened by the shoppers they send the email to? (Yes, they should know the answer to that question.) Do you include photos of the items for sale in the email or do you only send out a written description of the items that will be for sale?

Emails sent by your estate liquidator should also link back to their websites, where shoppers can be further enticed to go to your estate sale by viewing even more pictures and where they will get the chance to read expanded descriptions about what is being offered at your sale.

Make sure that they list your sale either on Craigslist or estatesales.net. These two listing services function very much today like newspaper classified advertising once did in the past.

10 WHAT IF I CHANGE MY MIND AND WANT TO RETAIN A FEW ITEMS AFTER WE HAVE SIGNED A CONTRACT?

Estate liquidators, as much as the best of them want to help, need to have financial incentives in place to encourage them to take on your project. These financial incentives mostly come down to their perceived understanding of the aggregate value of the items left in the home after family members have retained whatever it is they are going to retain. In their contracts, they are going to ask you to agree in writing to not remove anything from the home after the contract has been signed. Many estate liquidators have a clause in their contracts that stipulates that if you or any family member removes any item from the home after the contract has been signed, the estate will be charged whatever the commission on the item might have been. This is a normal standard operating procedure.

Retaining items, especially highly valuable items, can also have the consequence of negatively impacting a liquidator's ability to get shoppers to your sale. If there are not enough high-value items left in a home because a family has retained too many of them, an estate liquidator won't have enough of a sale left to promote.

Make sure that you go over this point with the liquidator you are thinking of hiring and fully understand what their policies are regarding the keeping of items after a contract has been signed. Under no circumstances should you rely on verbal agreements about this. Get all understandings in writing.

11 CAN WE PLACE PRICE RESERVES ON CERTAIN ITEMS?

Auction houses do this and many estate liquidation companies will also allow you to place reserves on certain items. The trick here is that this has

Even though most of us have gone digital, and, in fact, it's even hard to find real film these days, many people still collect old cameras.

to be done wisely. If you put reserves on too many items, then your sale will suffer; shoppers have to believe that they are getting deals or they won't buy. And on the flip side, you and your family want to have a sense of protection. No one in your family wants to see an item of great worth sold for just a few dollars, so yes, ask that reserves be placed on a limited number of items.

Doing this will also have the effect of opening up a deeper conversation between you and the estate liquidator about how they see value and what they think many of your best objects are worth.

If you are adamant that everything in the estate is fabulously valuable and that hundreds of items there will require reserves, then you are likely going to have a difficult time negotiating a contract with an estate liquidator, so be reasonable with them. Asking that reserves be placed on certain items is not an unheard of practice and if reserves are moderately applied, it's a win for both sides.

12 WHAT EXACTLY DO YOUR FEES COVER— ARE THERE ANY HIDDEN COSTS?

There are likely three fees you may encounter when dealing with an estate liquidator that, once explained, will make perfect sense to you:

SET UP AND SALES FEE: This fee should cover all the activities of setting up the house and making it ready for an estate sale, the estate liquidator's promotional efforts on the estate's behalf, and any staffing cost they may incur while conducting your estate sale. The most typical fee for this part of their service will be in the 30 to 35 percent range, but this fee can go up or down depending on your geographical location, value of your estate, or the overall difficulty of your project.

CREDIT CARD PROCESSING FEES: In the past, most estate liquidators weren't set up to accept credit cards, but that is slowly changing because consumers increasingly want to be able to use their credit cards to make their purchases. Of course, this makes buying easier for them, but it does add a layer of expense to the estate liquidator of between 2.75 to 5 percent of the total purchase. The good news for you is that by accepting credit cards, estate liquidators are greatly adding to the income potential of a sale. However, some companies may want to pass that cost onto the estates that they represent.

PRE OR POST ESTATE SALE DEBRIS REMOVAL FEES: Most estate liquidators will offer you the optional service of removing household items that they could not sell or donate to a landfill. Removing these unwanted, unusable, or unsalable items from a home could happen either just before the estate sale occurs or more commonly just after the estate sale takes place. This cost should be included as a line item in your contract.

13 DOES YOUR COMPANY PROVIDE A POST ESTATE SALE INVENTORY OF ALL ITEMS SOLD?

It is truly surprising how many companies don't include a post estate sales inventory that details the items they have sold on your behalf, although some do. If knowing with some degree of specificity which items were sold and for how much money is important to you, make sure to ask the liquidator that you are interviewing for a copy of one of their past estate sales inventories.

Most of these that you see will be fairly simple line item inventories. No estate liquidator is going to write long descriptions about the items which were sold, so you will have to read between the lines in order to get the fullest sense about how well separate items fared during the estate sales processes.

14 HOW LONG DOES IT TAKE FOR YOUR COMPANY TO SETTLE ITS ACCOUNTS AND SEND A CHECK TO THE ESTATE?

I've heard of estate liquidation companies that are able to get a check out to their clients in a day or two following an estate sale, but this is not the norm. In general, the busier an estate liquidator is, the more time they'll take to reconcile the estate sale that they've conducted for you.

If they are the type of estate liquidator that combines consignments from other estates within someone else's sale, then this is also something that can lead to a bit of delay. Even given such complications, an estate liquidation company should be able to generate a statement and issue a check to you in no longer than eighteen calendar days.

Make sure that this detail is in your contract.

15 CAN WE SEE A SAMPLE CONTRACT?

No matter what an estate liquidator verbally promises they will accomplish on your behalf, it's important to remember that if it isn't in the contract, they are not legally bound to do anything they promised.

I am not saying that they won't follow through on their verbal commitments, most will, it's just that they are not legally obligated to—so you want to make sure that you have a signed contract with a reputable firm before giving over your keys and permissions to allow them to enter the house. It's just common sense to do this.

Most estate liquidators will come to your home prepared to do business and will bring a contract with them and show it to you sometime near the end of their visit.

You might be in such a hurry to get through the whole process that you are anxious to sign their contract right then and there, but I advise you to get a copy of their contract, take it home with you and read it. Ask your attorney if they should also review it.

Don't succumb to hard sell pressure tactics that some estate liquidators might apply to get you to sign their contract before you are ready. And under no circumstance should you agree to have anyone do an estate sale for you without a signed contract.

16 WHAT MAKES YOUR ESTATE LIQUIDATION COMPANY DIFFERENT FROM YOUR COMPETITORS?

The six biggest resources an estate liquidator can show you to prove how much better their company is from their competitors are:

- Trained and dedicated staff
- Examples of past successes
- Use of results-driven mailing list
- Richly informative websites
- Letters from past clients with phone numbers
- Clear and easy to understand contracts

If you are talking to a company that can demonstrate that it has the above six resources firmly in place, then you are speaking with a rare estate liquidator and one you should seriously consider retaining. Most liquidators, while they may be working on acquiring these, won't have all five.

A great estate liquidator will be so secure about their services that when you ask them about their competitors, what you are more than likely going to hear from them are the various strengths of those competitors.

A great estate liquidator has plenty of business and never tries to get more of it by throwing mud on the efforts of others. My suggestion to you is to avoid liquidators who too readily speak ill of their competitors. You are looking for, and only want to work with, skilled professionals, not gossips or people who are jealous of the successes of others.

17 WE HAVE CERTAIN HIGH-VALUE ITEMS IN THE HOUSE, HOW WILL YOU SELL THESE ITEMS?

There are three basic kinds of estate liquidators who will:

- Research values a little, if at all, before selling
- Research values a lot before selling
- Research values, as well as sales venues, before selling

RESEARCH VALUES A LITTLE, IF AT ALL, BEFORE SELLING: These are estate liquidation companies that primarily see themselves as "liquidators" first. Their goal is to empty a house as fast as they can. They will only pay scant attention to researching values, believing for the most part that they have been hired to empty a house quickly and make it ready for sale.

When you ask them the question about high-value items, their answer may sound general and vague. If you are certain that you do not have high-end items in your home, then using the services of a firm like this will work out fine.

RESEARCH VALUES A LOT BEFORE SELLING: This is the category of estate liquidator who will most definitely take the time to research items that they feel have significant values. Many of these types of liquidators also have well trained staff members who are ever vigilant to surprises and are adept at finding them. These liquidators really don't like the label of "liquidator," preferring instead the professional application of "estate sales professionals."

When you ask them the above question about how they will value and sell high-valued items, their answers will be much clearer. Many of these people will let you know not only about the research sources they use, but also about how they have spent years developing relationships with local appraisers and specialists—professionals who they can rely on to quickly provide useful and relevant information regarding a great many categories of antiques and collectibles.

RESEARCH VALUES, AS WELL AS SALES VENUES, BEFORE SELLING: Here in a nutshell is the entire strategy or formula that I, as an estate sales professional, use to best approach the question of how to sell the contents of high-value estates or single high-value items that I may find in one.

Value determines venue and venue will either depreciate or enhance value. It's a new era in the estate sales business. It's no longer a given that the best of the best will be found by a fancy auctioneer while consulting with clients about an estate. Now more than ever, estate liquidators are getting calls from people who have mysterious and potentially valuable treasures. Maybe it's because of shows like PBS's *Antiques Roadshow* or others like it that people are diligently searching through their attics and basements for treasures. Or maybe it's because a whole lot of fresh material is coming onto the market because baby boomers are starting to age and are moving out of larger family homes into smaller more manageable spaces.

The reality is that because more people are becoming aware of how valuable some items found in a home can be, they now need the services of a new class of estate liquidator, one who understands the complex world of selling personal property via multiple sales channels. There is no one-size-fits-all approach. There are now multiple approaches and the best one to use is the one that is tailor made for the particulars of each individual estate.

Ask yourself how the answers to your questions compare to the answers you received from other estate liquidation companies.

Some estate liquidators are getting better at their trade and generating higher incomes for their clients, and the ranks of estate liquidators who are employing multiple sales venue strategies is growing. These estate liquidators are sending items for their clients to auction, creating relationships with national buyers, as well as conducting estate sales for the rest of the stuff that is in the home.

High-level estate liquidators know that while you could sell a Picasso painting at an estate sale, to do so would be utter madness. The reason is because auctions are the best place to sell high-valued items. So quietly, almost unknown to the average estate liquidator, an elite level of estate liquidator has been gaining the sort of respect once only available to major auctioneers. They are doing this by establishing a verifiable track record and holding themselves to the highest professional standards.

So, if you have high-value items that are part of your estate and you want to include them as part of the overall package you are agreeing to have sold on your behalf by an estate liquidator, make sure you choose a liquidator who has a proven track record. Ask them for documentation showing that they have successfully brought to market highly valuable paintings, collectibles or antiques.

A Note About Our Photographs

IN EVERY AMERICAN HOME, no matter the neighborhoods, where they were built, or the way their painted surfaces might meet the wondering eyes of neighbors, there is an interior world—a sanctuary with a familial atmosphere all its own.

This is what I am attempting to visually honor with my photographs—that people lived in those homes, and that these were the items in their processions at the moment of a life-changing transition.

Every home is different; who lived there, what they might have owned, and what they might have been trying to express themselves via their possessions is different. By focusing my lens in certain ways, I want to give shoppers who are thinking of coming to one of our estate sales a sense of the individual who lived there, and how what they owned was cherished by them, sometimes for decades.

I especially adore taking photographs of the many vignettes within our clients' homes, from their antique doll collections gathered together on a bed, each with a story to tell, to the leather-bound books stacked tall on their wooden bookshelves. When I look into a china cabinet, I wonder about a family's many gatherings, Christmas time and holidays filled with joy, love and laughter; their table set so elegantly with crystal and silver. To me, my photographs of a person's personal property document the way one generation of a family has handed down and shared its legacy with another.

It's my nature to take my time when I photograph items and to give care to respectfully conveying that though years have elapsed since the day this family moved into this house, that here lived people who loved and cherished the security and sanctity of the home they were able to have had the good fortune to create.

Their treasured items, now that they have been photographed, will be sold during their estate sale and will find their ways into new homes, with new families, and the process of love and cherishing will have a chance to continue for many generations to come.

Valetta Ciarla-Codina

Resources

The following sources can provide more information on estate sales and liquidation, appraisals, and some common areas of antiques and collectibles:

ESTATE SALES AND LIQUIDATION

http://finesf.com and **fineestateliquidation.com:** Author Martin Codina's websites. In addition to various articles about the business, there is a section that has an alphabetical listing of different antiques and collectibles and connects you to more than 500 experts in the field. You can also email him at: info@finesf.com.

estatesales.net: More than 2,000 estate liquidators in the U.S. regularly list on this site, and these companies account for as many as 4,000 estate sales each month. Besides finding estate sales listings, there are also tag sales and auction listings. Subscribers receive free weekly updates about sales near them.

estatesales.org: This site is a comprehensive resource for finding estate sales in your local area, and also provides tools for estate liquidators to market their sales online.

estatesales.com: Many estate liquidators list their sales on this site, which also provides various links to estate appraisals and estate planning.

ANTIQUES AND COLLECTIBLES, AND APPRAISALS

When tasked with liquidating an estate, you may come across objects and have no idea if they're an antique or collectible, or worth anything. The following websites are a good place to begin your research.

antiques.about.com and **collectibles.about.com:** These two sites offer helpful information about what items are popular in the world of antiques and collectibles. There are many other links located on these pages that lead to specific areas, such as glass and pottery.

www.pbs.org/wgbh/roadshow/: The online site of *Antiques Roadshow.* There are a number of useful sections including tips of the trade articles. You can also look up specific categories, from antiquities to tribal art.

www.appraisers.org/: American Society of Appraisers. Visit this site to find an expert appraiser in your area.

krausebooks.com: You can find a variety of antiques and collectibles books, including staples *Antique Trader Price Guide* and *Warman's Antiques & Collectibles Price Guide*, and books on coins, records, jewelry, glassware, pottery and toys.

Index

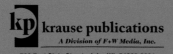